## ON THE COURT WITH . . .

# STEPHEN CURRY

ON THE COURT WITH . . .

# STEPHEN CURRY

## MATT CHRISTOPHER®

### The #1 Sports Series for Kids

### Text by Sam Page

**LITTLE, BROWN AND COMPANY**
New York   Boston

Little, Brown and Company
Hachette Book Group
1290 Avenue of the Americas, New York, NY 10104
Visit us at lb-kids.com
mattchristopher.com

First Edition: May 2017

Little, Brown and Company is a division of Hachette Book Group, Inc.
The Little, Brown name and logo are trademarks of Hachette Book Group, Inc.

The publisher is not responsible for websites (or their content) that are not owned by the publisher.

Matt Christopher® is a registered trademark of Matt Christopher Royalties, Inc.

Text written by Sam Page

ISBNs: 978-0-316-50958-9 (pbk.), 978-0-316-50955-8 (ebook)

Printed in the United States of America

LSC-C

10 9 8 7 6 5 4 3 2 1

# Contents

# ✶ CHAPTER ONE ✶

## 1988–1999

## The Early Charlotte Years

To get a sense of Stephen Curry's NBA career, take a peek at the back of his basketball card. To get a sense of Stephen Curry's childhood, take a look at his dad's.

Dell Curry played sixteen seasons in the NBA, earning a reputation—much like his son would one day—as a deadeye three-point shooter. In the spring of 1988, however, Dell was just a twenty-three-year-old shooting guard playing his second professional season with the Cleveland Cavaliers. That explains why, on March 14, 1988, Wardell Stephen Curry II was born in Akron, Ohio, the hometown of his one-day on-court rival LeBron James. That night, Dell scored fifteen points against the Knicks at Madison Square Garden and hit the only trey he attempted—a good omen for his son.

Stephen's mother, Sonya, was herself a great athlete. A three-sport star in high school, she played volleyball at Virginia Tech, where she met Dell. Many fans make the obvious connection between Stephen's and Dell's

1

skills on the court. (Dell ranked in the top ten in NBA three-point percentage in seven different seasons.) But in the ways he surpassed his father as a player, Stephen owes a lot to his mom.

"A lot of people say whatever defensive abilities I have, I get from her," Stephen once told a reporter. "My toughness and grittiness."

The off-season following Dell's one year with the Cavaliers, the newly formed Charlotte Hornets took him as their first pick in the 1988 expansion draft. Sonya, Dell, and baby Stephen moved to North Carolina, where they would spend the next decade. During that time, the family would see the birth of Stephen's younger brother, Seth (now a point guard for the Dallas Mavericks), and his younger sister, Sydel (a volleyball player at Elon University). In those ten years, Dell would score 9,839 points, still the most in Hornets franchise history.

Though they produced two NBA players, Stephen's parents made sure no one felt the pressure to follow in Dad's footsteps. Faith and academics always came first in their house. In fact, when Stephen was a first grader in 1995, his parents founded Christian Montessori School of Lake Norman, which Sonya still runs. There, Stephen learned with his family all around. He and Seth were in a class taught by his aunt India Adams. His grandmother, Candy Adams, was the school's cook.

With Dad playing basketball, Mom had to handle discipline at school and at home. She did not allow her kids to go to Dad's games during the week, or they would be out until eleven o'clock on a school night. She once made Stephen miss one of his own middle school games; she called her son's coach to explain that he had not washed the dishes.

When he got on the court, however, Stephen showed some of the traits that now make him an NBA superstar. At age six, he joined the Flames, his local rec center's team. With Stephen bombing from deep, they never lost. Like his dad on the Hornets, little Stephen had the ability to heat up from behind the three-point line.

The team was so good that they changed their name to the Stars and eventually advanced to the ten-and-under national championships held at Disney World in Orlando. In the tournament's title game, the Stars faced off against the Potomac Valley Blue Devils, who rallied late to take the lead. Down three points with one offensive possession left, the Stars called a time-out, during which the coach drew up a play meant to get Stephen open for a three-pointer. He got the shot off, and the defenders had to foul him to preserve their lead. Now a 90 percent free-throw shooter in the NBA who regularly leads the league in that category, he stepped to the line for three attempts. He had to make all three. The first shot missed.

"It was a moment that defined my childhood," Stephen would later tell *Sports Illustrated*. "It was all I thought about for a year. I felt I could go one of two ways afterward. I could run from that moment or I could want it again. I decided I wanted it."

Stephen played other sports, too, including baseball and football. Still, the idea of following in his father's footsteps proved irresistible, and he put hoops above the rest. Appearing with his dad in a Burger King commercial as "Dell Curry & Son," little Stephen told his dad he wanted to be a basketball player when he grew up. "Boy...that's going to take a lot of hard work and practice," Dell tells his son in the ad. "You've got to study hard, too."

"I know," Stephen replies. Turns out, he wasn't kidding.

# ★ CHAPTER TWO ★

## 1999-2002

### O Canada

Dell Curry did something during the lockout-shortened 1998–1999 NBA season that not even Stephen has accomplished: he led the league in three-point percentage, making 47.6 percent of his shots from behind the arc. That performance allowed him to sign a multiyear deal with the Toronto Raptors. The Currys were going to Canada!

The move proved a great opportunity for Dell—he had never made the playoffs with the Hornets, and the Raptors were a team on the rise. It also gave Stephen a chance to hang out with budding stars like Vince Carter and Tracy McGrady. He even shot around with his future Golden State Warriors coach Mark Jackson.

Though small, Stephen impressed his dad's teammates. Despite having over a foot in height on him, Alvin Williams remembers guarding Stephen tightly at professional three-point distance. Vince Carter finished his pregame workouts with a one-on-one game with Stephen.

"He had it all then," Carter would later recall in a TV interview, when he and Stephen were playing against each other in the NBA. "His mindset was, 'This time, I'm going to beat you.'"

While Stephen got to meet stars on his dad's team, he became a star at his new school. Now a thousand miles from North Carolina, the state that produced Michael Jordan, Stephen stood out as an eighth grader. Queensway Christian College did not have a very good middle school basketball team. His coach at Queensway, James Lackey, remembers Stephen's game being so far ahead of his peers' that he would bloody their noses in practice with passes they weren't expecting him to make. But with Stephen and Seth manning the backcourt together, the Saints went undefeated.

That is not to say Canada provided no competition for the Curry brothers. During one game against Hillcrest Junior Public School, bigger opponents slowed Stephen down. When Lackey called a time-out with a minute left and his team down by six, he seemed all but willing to give up. Then Stephen piped up.

"Give me the ball and we will win," Stephen said.

"You heard him," Lackey told the team. "Give him the ball and get out of his way."

His teammates did as they were told, and Stephen

delivered. He fired off a series of deep buckets, and the Saints didn't just win—they won easily.

While living in Toronto, Stephen also joined an all-star travel team called the 5-0. They went 33–4 and won the local championship. Stephen's legend in Canada grew after each spectacular performance. During one game, Stephen missed the first half while attending a Raptors practice, and the 5-0 trailed. He came into the game without warming up and made a three. During another contest, he had the "hot hand" that would later make him a must-watch superstar in the NBA. He seemed to make every shot, ending up with sixty-three points.

"I had to get out of there," Dell would later tell *Sports Illustrated*. "I felt bad for the other team. I couldn't watch what he was doing to those kids."

Stephen's days as a big fish in a small pond would not last forever, though. By the time he was nearly ready for high school, his dad's career was winding down. In the 2002 NBA playoffs, the Raptors faced off against the Detroit Pistons. After going down 0–2 in the series early, Toronto evened the series in two games at home. In the deciding Game 5 in Detroit, Dell led the Raptors in points with seventeen, despite playing only twenty-two minutes. He went a perfect three for three from behind the arc, including a shot with eleven seconds left in the game that put Toronto within two points of tying. The elder Curry's heroics were not enough, however, as the Pistons won, 85–82. Dell had played one of his most memorable games, and his last.

With no job holding them in Toronto, the Currys moved back to Charlotte, where Stephen, Seth, and Sydel attended high school. Playing basketball once again in North Carolina would be a challenge for Stephen, but also an opportunity. Many of the nation's top college basketball programs are in the area, including Duke, North Carolina State, and the University of North Carolina. Trying to earn a scholarship from a top university would be the next step toward Stephen's NBA dream.

# ⋆ CHAPTER THREE ⋆

## 2002–2005

### Making Varsity

Stephen Curry did not play varsity basketball his freshman year at Charlotte Christian School. That fact seems crazy now, given his superstardom. As a high school freshman, LeBron James stood at six feet, two inches and weighed 185 pounds, nearly the exact height and weight at which Stephen plays in the NBA now. But at the same age, Stephen stood at just five feet, six inches—and he was skinny. The player who would one day be known as the Baby-Faced Assassin looked, at the time, like a little kid.

Shonn Brown, the coach of the Charlotte Christian Knights, thought keeping Stephen on the junior varsity team would help him learn to be a leader. When Stephen finally did get a crack at varsity, he made a good impression. As a late season call-up, Stephen subbed into a game the Knights were losing in the first round of the state tournament. He sunk his first shot—a three-pointer, of course. Brown turned to his assistant coaches and told them they would give Stephen "the keys to our program."

As a sophomore, however, Stephen was not quite ready to take those keys. At that time, he did not resemble Stephen Curry, NBA superstar, in several important ways. He stood just five feet, eight inches, an improvement from his freshman year but still short for a basketball player. Unsure of his place on the team, he did not demand to play in the big moments. And, most crucially, Stephen lacked the effortless jump shot for which he is now famous.

Due to his size, Stephen had developed an unorthodox shooting form. He started with the ball at his hip and heaved it toward the hoop. He probably could have continued to get away with that technique in high school. His dad knew, however, that if Stephen wanted to play in college and eventually the pros, he would need a shot that taller opponents could not so easily block.

Stephen took his dad's advice to heart. But the switch was not easy. Since his earliest days in Charlotte to his dominant middle school career in Toronto, Stephen's shooting had always been his special talent, what set him apart from other kids. Now everything he knew about what he did best had to be unlearned. The summer of 2004, before his junior year, Stephen worked with Dell to develop new mechanics.

"It was tough for me to watch: them in the backyard, late nights, a lot of hours during the day, working on his shot," Seth Curry said in an ESPN interview. "They broke it down to a point where he couldn't shoot at all. He'd be back there at times crying, not wanting to work on his game. He had to do it rep, after rep, after rep, to a point where he was able to master it."

For weeks, Stephen had a hard time making a shot outside of the paint, much less from deep. At camps, his peers wondered why a short kid who couldn't even shoot was trying to play basketball. Focused on his ultimate goal of becoming an NBA star, however, Stephen endured that tough summer and worked hard on the improvements his dad had suggested. While he was tempted to show those other kids that he could score by using his old shot, he persevered.

By the time school started again, Stephen had figured out the form that would make him famous. The ball starts above his eyes, well out of the reach of would-be shot blockers. Then, needing just a flick of the wrist, it leaves his hands before defenses can react, taking a route to the hoop more like a rainbow than a line drive.

Coach Brown recognized how hard Stephen had worked that summer, and he told the junior to take charge of the team. Stephen's leadership really shined during a tournament that Charlotte Christian entered as an underdog. The Bojangles' Shootout, hosted by none other than Dell Curry, was an annual competition held for the best teams in the area. The Knights' first big upset win came against West Charlotte, a powerhouse ranked fourth in the area by the local newspaper (Charlotte Christian was unranked). Known for their full-court press, West Charlotte had no answer for Stephen Curry, who had twenty-two points and seven rebounds in an 85–79 win.

In the next game, Stephen had an even more impressive twenty-five points, five rebounds, five steals, and four blocks in a 73–59 win against another ranked team, eighth-seed Gaston Day. That win earned them a spot in the championship game against twelfth-seed Victory Christian. Stephen's numbers weren't as good that time: he scored just eleven points. But the Knights settled down after giving up eight unanswered points at the start of the game and won, 62–55. Stephen was named the tournament MVP.

The Shootout validated Stephen's hard work the summer before and established his and Charlotte Christian's reputations in the area. More importantly, however, it gave Stephen a chance to impress coaches from top college programs, some of whom had watched his heroics from the crowd.

A month after the tournament, Stephen took an official visit to Virginia Tech, the school where his dad had played basketball and his mom had played volleyball. Following in his parents' footsteps seemed like a fitting next step for Stephen. But like so much else in his career, the recruiting process would not prove that easy.

# ★ CHAPTER FOUR ★

## 2005-2006

### Recruitment and Graduation

Believe it or not: Stephen Curry had a bad game.

The summer after his junior year, Stephen had a busy schedule meant to showcase his talents for the country's top college recruiters. On a travel team coached by his dad, Stephen set out for Las Vegas to play a tournament against elite competition. But with college coaches in the crowd, Stephen didn't play well. He worried that his entire basketball dream would unravel as a result, asking his mom after the game, "Did I mess up?"

"My heart just broke," Sonya told the *San Francisco Chronicle.* "It was a learning lesson for me as a parent, to just back up and let it be."

The sad truth was that Stephen did not hurt his chances to impress those big-time coaches, because he never had any chance at all. Ultimately, they had trouble looking past his size. Stephen had a reputation as a kid who, while he had his father's talent for shooting, was probably too small and too soft to play at the highest collegiate level.

"I don't ever remember even seeing him," UNC coach Roy Williams would tell ESPN in hindsight. "I do know that when I did see him I thought, 'Man, he is little.'"

Stephen had visited Virginia Tech earlier that year, but even their coaches did not seem that enthusiastic about signing up Dell Curry's son. They ultimately offered him a spot as a walk-on. In other words, they did not think he was good enough for a full scholarship yet. While Stephen did not complain about this disappointment, his brother, Seth, could tell it bothered him. He channeled those frustrations into more hard work and hoped that the right school would still come along.

The right school turned out to be Davidson College, located just twenty miles north of Charlotte. Before Stephen arrived at Davidson, the Wildcats had appeared in the NCAA Tournament just seven times ever. UNC made thirty-seven March Madness appearances in the same span. Davidson had produced five NBA players before Stephen Curry. Eighty-three former Tar Heels have gone pro, four of whom are now in the Hall of Fame.

Davidson head coach Bob McKillop got to watch Stephen Curry early on. McKillop's son played baseball with Stephen when they were ten years old. Whether he was patrolling centerfield or dribbling in the paint, Stephen's athleticism and talent stood out. McKillop believes now that Stephen could have become a Major League Baseball standout if he had chosen baseball instead.

While other coaches doubted Stephen's potential, McKillop saw a rising star. He pursued Stephen aggressively in high school, writing him supportive e-mails after games and practices. McKillop noticed intangible traits other coaches missed: Stephen's toughness in the face of bigger opponents, his attention to detail, and his tireless work ethic.

In September 2005, McKillop visited the Curry home, and Stephen committed to Davidson. Sonya Curry walked to the door with McKillop as he left. Aware of what other colleges had thought of her son, she tried to assure the coach that Stephen would be ready for the rigors of NCAA ball.

"Okay, Coach, I'm going to fatten him up for you," Sonya said.

"I'll take him just the way he is," McKillop replied.

Sonya Curry cried tears of relief.

Before his college career started, however, Stephen had the small matter of his senior season at Charlotte Christian to get out of the way. The Knights reached new heights in Stephen's final year, making a big statement at the annual Chick-fil-A Classic in South

Carolina. Drawing from the best talent in the Southeast, the Classic gave Stephen a chance to play against some of the nation's top teams.

The Knights almost didn't make it out of the first round. Against Lower Richland, a team from South Carolina, they were down eleven points at halftime. Then Stephen did something that would become his trademark: he got hot from deep, shooting his team out of a hole. After registering just four points in the first half, Stephen scored twenty. With five minutes left, Stephen hit a trey to bring Charlotte Christian within three. He then hit another three—tie game. He made another shot to put his team up two, the margin in a 58–56 victory. The Knights ultimately won the tournament, upsetting Norcross, a top team from Georgia, in the finals. Stephen earned MVP honors.

Next came the Knights' shot to repeat as champions in Dell Curry's Bojangles' Shootout. This time, they could not play the role of the plucky underdogs. Undefeated and top-ranked, Charlotte Christian was the team to beat. With bandages on his head—the result of too much pregame jumping around—Curry did it all in the championship game: fifteen points, fifteen rebounds, eight steals, and seven assists. He was named the tournament MVP for the second year in a row.

In the state finals that February, foul troubles kept Stephen on the bench for much of the game, and the

Knights lost. With his high school legacy secure, however, that game only proved his importance to the team. Stephen graduated with multiple school records, including career three-pointers made (170) and steals (232). Even more impressively, he set these marks despite playing varsity for just three years!

More important than his on-court achievements was his work in the classroom. Teachers remember Stephen as a humble, focused, and respectful pupil. Even with his college future secured by his Davidson scholarship, Stephen worked hard, no matter what the class. That attitude—combined with a growth spurt that finally made him six feet tall—made him ready for the challenge of NCAA basketball.

# ⋆ CHAPTER FIVE ⋆

## 2006–2007

### Freshman Year

Stephen Curry got kicked out of his first college practice. He had shown up late, and Coach Bob McKillop told him to practice elsewhere that day. But after watching Stephen at practices for which he showed up on time—McKillop says Stephen was never late again—the Davidson coach knew he had a special player. He told Davidson alumni that the team had a player who could put the Wildcats on the map.

Still, there were growing pains. Davidson's first game of the 2006–2007 season was on the road against Eastern Michigan. Stephen started the game but struggled, turning the ball over nine times in just the first half of the game. The plays Stephen was used to getting away with in high school wouldn't work against seasoned college defenders. At halftime, Davidson trailed 44–28, but McKillop decided to stick with his freshman guard for the rest of the game. Stephen rewarded that faith, as the Wildcats came storming out of the locker room. Finally, with 2:35 left in the game, Stephen hit a three-pointer, and then another, to give his team a four-point lead. They won 81–77. Despite the bad habits he may have brought from high school, Stephen still had his penchant for clutch late-game threes.

"That's a great credit to him that he didn't hang his head," McKillop told the *Charlotte Observer* after the game. "You saw him do some things that show he's a pretty special player. He understands what it means to respond in tough situations, and he did."

Stephen made an even bigger statement in his second game. Playing against the more formidable University of Michigan, he scored seventeen points in the first half. The heavily favored Wolverines ultimately won, 78–68, but they had few answers for the skinny, unknown freshman, who finished the game with thirty-two points and nine rebounds.

For the rest of that opening month of November, Davidson beat up on weaker teams, while losing to major programs, such as Missouri and Duke. Against the top competition, Stephen struggled, surrendering ten turnovers versus Missouri and scoring zero points in the first half against Duke. Still, he had clearly established himself as his team's go-to scoring option and a player for whom other teams had to plan.

After the Duke loss, Davidson won twenty-two of their final twenty-three regular season games. Stephen

19

finished the season averaging 21.5 points per game, having shot 40.8 percent from behind the arc. He ranked second in the entire nation in freshman scoring. University of Texas forward Kevin Durant, the second overall pick in that summer's NBA draft and Stephen's future Golden State teammate, was the only first-year player to score more.

Davidson went 17–1 against their Southern Conference rivals that season. And there was little doubt about the reason for their dominance: Stephen's conference-leading 730 points were 125 more than the next best player. Fans had reason to wonder how a player as talented as Stephen had ended up in a mid-major conference in the first place.

On December 19, 2006, the day after Davidson beat Chattanooga 92–80 behind a thirty-point, eleven-rebound Curry performance, the local paper in Chattanooga printed a column on the front page of the sports section entitled GREENBERG SHOULD GET ALL THE BLAME. The writer reasoned that Virginia Tech coach Seth Greenberg had unleashed Stephen upon the Southern Conference when he didn't offer the point guard a full scholarship. The Chattanooga coach was quoted as having talked to Greenberg, who—just two months into Stephen's college career—already knew he had made a mistake. The paper figured that with Stephen around, "it's hard to imagine the Mocs advancing to the NCAA Tournament."

They were right. Davidson won the conference tournament, earning an automatic bid into the NCAA Tournament. The Wildcats earned the thirteenth seed, which pitted them against fourth-seed Maryland in the first round. For the first time since their loss to Duke, Stephen and his teammates had a chance to prove they could hang with the country's top teams. The game was billed as a matchup between the sons of two famous former athletes. D. J. Strawberry, the player tasked with guarding Curry, is the son of former MLB player Darryl Strawberry.

Davidson showed no hesitation despite being the lower seed. The teams played a back-and-forth first twenty minutes. With 3:24 remaining in the first half and his team trailing by one, Curry made a statement, pulling up for a deep three against seven-foot-one Will Bowers. The shot that Dell Curry had designed to never be blocked sailed right over the towering defender's head and into the hoop. "Are you kidding me?!" screamed a CBS announcer with a laugh. Though maybe the first, it would not be the last time Stephen Curry inspired disbelief playing on national television.

Coming out of halftime down, the Wildcats took a quick 52–44 lead after a 9–0 run, punctuated by a great pass from Stephen to set up a teammate's layup. It seemed as though an upset was in the works. The Terps came back soon with a run of their own and made big shots down the stretch. Guarded by Strawberry, Stephen went uncharacteristically cold, missing five of his final six shots. Maryland won, 82–70.

Still, Stephen had proved he and Davidson were a team on the rise. He had also shown the major programs that had not pursued him on account of his size what a mistake they had made. After the game, Maryland's coach told Stephen, "You could play anywhere." But he was playing for Davidson—and not as a "one-and-done" freshman who spends just a single season playing college ball before going pro. Stephen and the Wildcats would be back next season, and on a mission.

# ★ CHAPTER SIX ★

## 2007–2008

### The Calm Before the Storm

Stephen's sophomore season started familiarly, with a series of out-of-conference games against top schools. Coming into Stephen's second year, Coach McKillop challenged his team with a tougher schedule. Their opponents before the new year included the top two teams in the nation, UNC and the University of California, Los Angeles, along with perennial contenders Duke and NC State.

In his second game of the season, Stephen scored twenty-four points against first-seed UNC in a 72–68 loss. UNC coach Roy Williams, the one who found Stephen to be "little," became the latest coach to publicly admit underestimating Stephen during the recruiting process. Against Duke, the Wildcats avoided last year's rout but still lost 79–73, despite Stephen's twenty points. They then blew an eighteen-point first-half lead to Russell Westbrook's UCLA Bruins, eventually falling 75–63.

The closest Davidson got to beating a ranked team

was against NC State. With forty-three seconds left in the game, Stephen hit a three to put them up by one, 65–64. An NC State player responded by making two free throws to go up 66–65. Stephen took the last shot, a heave from half-court. It hit the rim.

The Wildcats couldn't find the signature upset they wanted. After their first ten games, they stood 4–6. Newspapers described their opponents as having "escaped" or "squeaked by." After all, a loss to a mid-major opponent like Davidson would have been a disaster for any of those teams. That was probably little consolation to Davidson. And to make matters worse, it came out that Stephen had been playing all season with a torn ligament in his left wrist, an injury that would eventually require surgery. He decided to play through the pain and wait until the off-season to get it fixed.

And play through it he did: Stephen dressed for all thirty-six regular season and conference tournament games. His 25.9 points-per-game average ranked fifth in the nation. Playing at shooting guard instead of point guard that season, he had more opportunities to get open and bomb away. Davidson went on a twenty-two-game winning streak to improve to 26–6. The Wildcats cracked a Top 25 poll for the first time since 1970 and earned another NCAA Tournament berth. Stephen Curry was headed back to the Big Dance to play in a tournament that would change his life.

# ★ CHAPTER SEVEN ★

## 2008

## March Madness

In tenth-seed Davidson's first-round NCAA Tournament game against seventh-seed Gonzaga, he was heating up. With an easy stroke, he shot three-pointer after three-pointer, starting out a perfect five-for-five from behind the arc. The only problem for Davidson: he wasn't Stephen Curry, the sharpshooter that had many people thinking the Wildcats could pull off the upset. The person hitting all these deep bombs was Steven Gray, Stephen's opposite on the Bulldogs.

The game was held in Raleigh, North Carolina, on the home court of NC State, where the Wildcats had lost by just one point in December. So close to Charlotte—and so far away from Gonzaga's home of Spokane, Washington—it was practically a Davidson home crowd. But Gonzaga had given them little reason to cheer, leading 28–17 almost thirteen minutes into the game.

Just when the game threatened to get out of hand, Stephen stepped up to make a trey of his own.

Immediately, the TV announcers marveled at the shot's hard-to-block arc and easy path to the hoop.

"Wow, is that sweet," said play-by-play man Jim Nantz. Well into Gonzaga's possession, they were still talking about the Davidson shooting guard's pleasing technique.

"Have you ever seen a softer three?"

"Beautiful."

Unfortunately for Stephen and the Wildcats, it was quantity, not quality, of shots that mattered in this game. Four minutes into the second half, Stephen had a clean breakaway, but he couldn't convert after a blatant foul from a Gonzaga defender. The referee made no call. On the ensuing Gonzaga possession, Stephen fell down, and his man took the opportunity to make an uncontested three. Once again, Davidson found themselves down eleven points, 54–43.

Every time Davidson made a little progress cutting into the score, Gonzaga had an answer. After getting within eight points, the Wildcats surrendered an easy baseline drive, which put the deficit at ten with less than fourteen minutes to go.

But on the next possession, Stephen caught Gonzaga napping and made a quick three in transition to cut the lead to eight. Gonzaga missed their next shot, and Davidson went right back to work on offense. Davidson point guard Jason Richards tried a three that clanked off the rim. In the ensuing chaos, the Wildcats got the offensive rebound and found a wide-open Stephen. *Bang!* Stephen had scored his team's last eleven points. The lead had shrunk from ten to four in an instant. The crowd came alive.

"They can't guard you," Richards told Curry. "They cannot guard you."

With a concerned look on her face, Sonya Curry stood up in the stands and waved a Davidson pom-pom. Dell Curry sat next to her in a red sweater-vest, the same color as his son's jersey. Occasionally he mouthed advice to Stephen.

With Gonzaga leading by five with 10:23 to go, Stephen again got the ball right in front of his team's bench, the spot where he had shot so well all half. Fearing another three, a Gonzaga defender nearly jumped out of his shoes going for the block. As composed as ever, Stephen simply allowed his opponent to fly by, dribbling in for an easy two-point field goal. The lead was just three.

The Bulldogs' attempt to answer missed, and Davidson came back up the floor. This time, Curry ran right behind a teammate who had the ball at the top of the key. Like a running back taking a pitch from his quarterback, Stephen caught the ball from several feet behind the three-point line and shot before anyone could react. The distance didn't bother him. He had "in the gym range"—it seemed as if he could hit from anywhere. *Swish*. Suddenly, the game that Gonzaga had led all day was tied.

From that point on, it was a back-and-forth contest. And with just 1:45 left, the score was once again tied, 74–74. Gonzaga was all over Stephen on defense. They guarded him close at any distance. So with just seventy-one seconds left in the game and one second on the shot clock, a teammate had to take the shot, which hit the back of the rim.

Somehow, despite being outnumbered two-to-one under the rim, Davidson's Andrew Lovedale came up with the rebound. Stephen, who had been getting back on defense, sprinted to the three-point line, where Lovedale found him unguarded. As soon as Stephen had the ball all alone, his teammates on the bench started to jump up and down. The whole crowd knew what came next. Stephen knocked down the biggest shot of his life as if it was just another warm-up jumper at practice. The game ended, 77–74.

Running back down the court, Stephen pointed to his mom and dad in the crowd, then straight up, to God. When Gonzaga's coach called a time-out to settle his team down, Stephen let his emotions feed off the crowd, jumping up and down.

Stephen made three free throws to secure the final score, 82–76. He had scored forty points, thirty of which had come in the second half. The kid who hadn't been chosen to follow in his father's footsteps at Virginia Tech had accomplished something his dad hadn't: he won a game in the NCAA Tournament.

"I'm not seeing so much of myself in him anymore," Dell said after the game. "I couldn't dribble that well. I wasn't as quick as he is. I think he's surpassed me."

Stephen hadn't just lived up to his family name, however. He was making a name of his own. Suddenly, the basketball world was watching Stephen Curry.

The Wildcats couldn't celebrate for long. Just two days later they had to face a much tougher team: the Georgetown Hoyas. The second seed in the tournament, Georgetown had one more win than Davidson on the season despite a much tougher schedule. They were ranked ninth nationally and led the country in field goal percentage defense. Beating them would vault Davidson to "Cinderella team" status.

It seemed like a long shot. Davidson didn't have a single player taller than six feet, nine inches. Roy Hibbert, a seven-foot-two senior, anchored the Hoyas. In many ways, he was Stephen's opposite: a player whose imposing physical stature landed him a spot on one of the most storied collegiate programs. A surefire NBA draft pick, he'd had the option to go pro the season before, after leading Georgetown to the Final Four. But he returned to college citing "unfinished business." In other words, he intended to win the tournament, and Stephen Curry was in his way.

After one half, it seemed as though Georgetown would blow past Davidson. The Hoyas led 38–27, which quickly became 43–27 when the teams returned from the locker rooms. Stephen had missed ten of his first twelve shots, scoring just five points. By contrast, everything seemed to be dropping for the opposition.

Stephen had managed to win in similar situations. Against Gonzaga in the first round, against Lower Richland in high school, against Hillcrest Junior as an eighth grader in Canada, he had found his touch in the game's most crucial moments. But against Georgetown? Down sixteen in the second half?

Stephen made a three-point play—despite being fouled—that brought the Wildcats within eleven, 48–37, with 14:24 on the clock. Davidson had been down ten with nearly the same amount of time left against Gonzaga. Stephen then used every skill that would one day make him an NBA MVP point guard. He hit two three-pointers and set up teammates with precise passes. At 8:47 left, he found Lovedale alone under the basket with a slick dish. That play punctuated a 16–2 run, which brought Davidson within two points, 50–48.

With 4:40 left, Stephen made a layup and one free throw, giving the Wildcats a 60–58 lead. After Georgetown tied it on the next possession, Stephen showed how unstoppable he could really be. Double-teamed, Stephen crossed over both defenders and dribbled the ball between them. With one trying to block his layup from behind and a third opponent trying to block it from the front, Stephen held the ball to the side in one hand and casually flipped it in the air for a scoop shot. It banked high off the glass and went in. He followed it up with another three, giving Davidson a 65–60 lead.

Down the stretch, Stephen made five out of six free throws to seal the win, 74–70. He had scored twenty-five points in the second half to give him thirty total for the game. Hibbert, who got into foul trouble early, played just sixteen minutes and scored six points.

As the final buzzer sounded, Davidson's players stormed center court, hugging and fist pumping. Photographers mobbed Stephen, who made his way to the Davidson fans in the arena, shouting out, "It's all of y'all!" As Stephen hugged her, Sonya Curry asked her son, "What the heck is going on?" When he went to watch North Carolina versus Arkansas later that day, Stephen wore a hoodie with BRACKETBUSTERS on the front.

"I'm numb right now," McKillop said. His team was headed to the Sweet 16.

There, Davidson met Wisconsin, one of the top defensive teams in college basketball. They had allowed, on average, fewer points than any other team in the nation. Michael Flowers, a senior known for guarding other team's stars, said before the game that he hoped to leave Stephen "breathless."

The key for Davidson was to not count on another big second half to bail them out. Two miraculous comebacks had been unlikely enough. They couldn't expect a third. And sure enough, they kept it close in the first half. After a back-and-forth twenty minutes with plenty of lead changes, the game was knotted up 36–36. Stephen made just four of his twelve attempts.

Despite his team not needing to be rescued, however, Stephen exploded in the second half for the third consecutive game. With less than fifteen minutes left, he made a bank shot for two. Wisconsin answered, but on the next possession, Stephen let Flowers run by him and knocked down an easy three. When the Badgers tried to respond on their next possession, Stephen stripped the ball, creating a two-on-one fast break down the court. After getting a pass from Richards, Curry calmly pump-faked, causing another overanxious defender to run right past him before draining another open trey.

Wisconsin threw the ball out of bounds, and Richards made a three of his own. A few possessions later, before the Badgers could score another point, Stephen knocked down a deep shot off the dribble. Before they could realize what had happened, Wisconsin was down by fifteen points. In three minutes and fifteen seconds, Davidson had gone on a 12–0 streak, bookended by Stephen Curry three-pointers.

Then, with just over nine minutes left, Stephen

delivered the dagger, and surprisingly not with a jumper. Streaking toward the basket undetected, Stephen pulled off an acrobatic reverse layup, his most impressive move in the entire tournament. The Davidson fans exploded. LeBron James, who had flown to Detroit specifically to watch Stephen play, couldn't hide his excitement. Davidson never let up in this game, winning 73–56. Stephen scored more points in the second half (twenty-two) than the entire Wisconsin team. The kid too skinny to play for the nation's best teams was now beating them almost single-handedly.

In the Elite Eight, Davidson drew the first-seed Kansas Jayhawks, a consensus top-five squad that had lost only three games all season. They had multiple players who could score, compared to Davidson who leaned heavily on Stephen.

The game was a defensive battle. The score remained tied 2–2 until 15:07, when Kansas made their second basket. Davidson made just one of their first ten attempts, as Stephen came out ice-cold. He started to make some shots, but the Jayhawks usually had an answer. Kansas led 30–28 at the half.

This time, there would be no second-half explosion from Stephen Curry. With twenty points early in the second half, Stephen scored just five in the final eighteen minutes of the game. But maybe it wouldn't matter, as Stephen's teammates picked him up, starting to make shots of their own. Bryant Barr, who had averaged just 5.3 points per game for Davidson that season, scored eleven. This team effort kept Davidson in the game late, trailing by just five, 59–54, with a minute to go.

Then, with fifty-five seconds on the clock, Stephen caught an inbound pass and threw up a three. *Swish!* 59–57. The Davidson magic was back, it seemed. With so much time on the clock, the Wildcats didn't need to foul. They started in a full-court press and played their opponents tight man-to-man. Unable to find a good shot, the Kansas players settled for a desperate three with the shot clock expiring. The ball hit the rim and went out of bounds. With 16.8 seconds, Davidson gained possession, with a chance for their most thrilling finish yet.

Curry dribbled the ball up the court. Ten seconds remaining. He faked as if he wanted to drive in, and then pulled back behind the three-point line. One defender fell over, while another picked him up. Six seconds. Coming around a screen, he couldn't shake a double-team. He pump-faked—only one of the two defenders bit. Three seconds. Completely covered, he passed the ball to Richards. His shot hit off the side of the backboard as the buzzer sounded. The run was over. Davidson had been two points away from advancing to the Final Four.

The Jayhawks would go on to win the tournament. No other team came as close to beating them as the Wildcats had.

# ✶ CHAPTER EIGHT ✶

## 2008–2009

### The Draft

Stephen Curry did not win the 2008 NCAA Tournament. But he and his teammates got closer than anyone ever expected them to. Even his parents, Dell and Sonya Curry, had driven back home from the tournament games in Raleigh in a stunned silence. Their son was now a household name.

Thanks to his March Madness stardom, Stephen was interviewed on *Late Night with Conan O'Brien* and ESPN. He appeared at the ESPY (Excellence in Sports Performance Yearly) awards, nominated for Best Breakthrough Athlete. More importantly, NBA fans began to covet Stephen for their favorite teams as a serious draft prospect. What team wouldn't want a three-point shooter of Stephen's caliber? Still, he decided to return for his junior year at Davidson.

In addition to the weight of expectations created by his March Madness run, Stephen had to navigate a position change in his third college season. With Jason Richards graduating, he moved from shooting guard to point guard. It made sense: Stephen was the best play-maker left on the team. But there was a practical consideration for his pro career. Shooting guards tend to be taller than point guards. At six feet, three inches, Stephen would look less out of place in the NBA as a shoot-first point guard than an undersized two guard.

The switch didn't seem to faze him. Stephen led the NCAA in scoring with 28.6 points per game. His assists also jumped, from 2.9 per game to 5.6, a reflection of his skill as a point guard. He finished his college career with a slew of NCAA and Davidson records, including the college's all-time scoring mark (2,635), which he broke in his second-to-last regular season game.

And he did all that in spite of one November contest against Loyola University Maryland, during which Stephen scored zero points. The opposing coach seemed more interested in stopping Davidson's star with a dedicated double-team than winning the game. Rather than force any shots (he attempted only three all game), Stephen merely passed to his teammates, who won the game by thirty. The Loyola coach drew criticism for his petty move, while Stephen garnered praise for his selfless play.

There would be no twenty-five-game win streak for

the Wildcats this season. They dropped three conference games, including a 59–52 loss to the College of Charleston in the Southern Conference tournament. Without the automatic bid they had earned the previous two seasons for being conference champs, Davidson had to campaign for a berth in the NCAA Tournament. They were denied. Instead, they lost in the second round of the National Invitation Tournament, a competition for teams who don't make the Big Dance. Stephen scored twenty-six points in his final college game.

After a stellar three years, Stephen declared for the 2009 NBA draft, promising to eventually return to school to finish his degree. He was projected as a sure-fire first-round pick, likely to be in the top ten. That didn't mean, however, the questions that had always dogged him about his size, toughness, and athleticism went away. Teams often choose physical potential over demonstrated ability in the draft. Players with questionable basketball skills regularly get picked because they're seven feet tall. In that kind of environment, the doubters of Stephen's ability to play at a higher level only grew louder.

"He doesn't have the upside of [Ricky] Rubio," said ESPN draft analyst Doug Gottlieb. "[Brandon] Jennings, [Jonny] Flynn, [Patty] Mills, [and Jeff] Teague [are] all more athletic."

Not being the first point guard picked seemed to suit Stephen. The New York Knicks had the eighth pick in the draft and a vacancy at the position. Knicks coach Mike D'Antoni preferred an up-tempo, high-scoring offense. New York demonstrated serious interest in Stephen, scheduling a predraft workout and sending team president Donnie Walsh to meet him at the Draft Combine.

The feeling turned out to be mutual. Stephen said playing for the Knicks would be "a dream come true" during an interview with a New York radio station. Rumors had even surfaced that Stephen's decision to forgo his senior season at Davidson had been prompted by a promise from the Knicks that they would pick him. (Stephen denied those reports.) Stephen's agent went so far as to decline an invitation to work out for the Memphis Grizzlies, who had the second pick.

It seemed as if the only obstacle to Stephen becoming the next big star at Madison Square Garden was the team picking directly before the Knicks: the Golden State Warriors. Golden State had a reputation as a poorly managed franchise. Dell Curry didn't like the personalities of some of the players in their locker room. Stephen did not meet with or work out for the Warriors management. Stephen's agent flat out told the team not to pick him.

As draft day approached, though, it seemed increasingly unlikely that Stephen would end up on the Knicks. A good combine performance and a promise not to hold out for a trade to New York caused his stock to rise. It seemed as if Stephen might now go in the top five, leaving New York and Golden State without their coveted point guard.

On June 25, 2009, the best basketball prospects in the world gathered at Madison Square Garden for the biggest night of their young lives. Stephen Curry sat in the green room with his parents, sister Sydel, and girlfriend Ayesha Alexander. Many of the Knicks fans in the audience hoped he would be staying in New York for more than just one night. With the first two picks in the draft, the Los Angeles Clippers and the Grizzlies took big men Blake Griffin and Hasheem Thabeet. At three and four, the Oklahoma City Thunder and Sacramento Kings took shooting guards James Harden and Tyreke Evans. No surprises so far.

Now it came time for the point guards to go. The Minnesota Timberwolves, thanks to a predraft trade, had the fifth and sixth picks. First they took Ricky Rubio, a Spanish player who had first gone pro in his home country at age fourteen. Renowned for his passing, Rubio had been projected to go ahead of Stephen.

Minnesota needed a player to pair with Rubio in

their backcourt. Given his experience playing both guard positions, Stephen seemed like a logical choice. Rubio could drop dimes that Stephen would convert to easy threes. In anticipation of his being picked, the TV cameras focused on Stephen, who was sitting patiently. But the Timberwolves selected Jonny Flynn, a point guard from Syracuse. The New York crowd cheered, though not necessarily for Flynn. Their Knicks still had a chance at Stephen.

The commissioner came to the podium again. "With the seventh pick in the 2009 NBA draft, the Golden State Warriors select...Stephen Curry from Davidson College." The crowd erupted in a scream of collective anguish, followed by deafening boos.

Sorry, Knicks fans. Stephen Curry was a Warrior— but for how long? Almost as soon as the pick happened, reports came out of a possible trade that would send Phoenix Suns power forward Amar'e Stoudemire to Golden State for Stephen, among other assets. Steve Kerr, who would one day coach Stephen on the Warriors, was the Suns general manager at the time. He supposedly liked Curry as a long-term replacement for Steve Nash.

"I hope I go to sleep a Warrior," Stephen said when asked about the trade rumors that evening.

The deal, of course, never happened. Stephen flew to Oracle Arena to be introduced. At the press conference, he praised his new team, saying it was a great fit for him. General manager Larry Riley emphasized his new point guard's strong family background and assured the media that no trade was coming.

"He can unpack his bags, go look for a house, and relax," Riley said. "He ain't going anyplace."

The Stephen Curry era in Oakland had officially begun.

# ⋆ CHAPTER NINE ⋆

## 2009–2011

## Welcome to the NBA

"Us together? No."

That was Warriors guard Monta Ellis's reaction when asked about sharing a backcourt with Stephen Curry. A second-round pick in the 2005 draft, the twenty-four-year-old Ellis had blossomed into Golden State's star scorer, averaging 19.9 points per game from 2007–2009. Ellis had found success by shooting a lot. Now, faced with the possibility of playing with a physically similar player (Ellis, like Curry, is six feet, three inches), a player who took plenty of shots of his own, he wasn't happy. To make matters worse, the team's other leading scorer, Stephen Jackson, demanded a trade.

Stephen, meanwhile, was working hard to reward the Warriors' faith in him by working hard to prepare physically for the eighty-two-game season. He signed a four-year, $12.7 million rookie contract and a shoe deal with Nike. When Stephen did arrive for Warriors training camp, he graciously brushed Ellis's comments aside.

"He has experience," Stephen said. "And he knows how to win, what it's going to take. So if that's what he sees, then there's got to be some validity to it."

Ever humble, Stephen always took the high road. If something was bothering him—not playing for the Knicks, his teammate's lukewarm reception—he never let it show. When it finally came time to play basketball, Stephen impressed. Warriors coach Don Nelson praised Stephen's work in practice. And in exhibition games, Stephen showed off the solid passing and defense that were often overshadowed by his shooting in college. Nelson indicated Curry would start at least part-time.

On October 28, 2009, the Warriors hosted the Houston Rockets for their first game of the year. Stephen started at point guard and brought the ball up for the contest's first possession. He executed a pick-and-roll with Jackson, finding the forward under the basket for an easy layup. Stephen had his first NBA assist. Two minutes later, Stephen came off another pick to get an easy look from the free-throw line. He had scored the first two points of many in his NBA career.

In true Stephen Curry fashion, he tried to ignite a fourth-quarter comeback for the Warriors. Down

108–101 with a minute and a half to go, Curry scored six quick points, but it wasn't enough. The Warriors lost, 108–107. Stephen finished the game with an impressive stat line: fourteen points, seven assists, and four steals.

That loss would be the first of many that season for the Warriors. Injuries and illness plagued the team. That meant a poor win-loss record, but also plenty of opportunities for Stephen to play and get experience. During one January game against the Milwaukee Bucks, Stephen committed six fouls, which would normally cause a player to foul out. The Warriors had so few players, however, they could not replace Stephen and the rules allowed him to finish the game. He played all forty-eight minutes for the first time in his career.

A month later, Stephen recorded his first triple-double at home against the Clippers with thirty-six points, thirteen assists, and ten rebounds. He was the first NBA rookie to have at least thirty points, ten assists, and ten rebounds since 1988. His performance allowed the Warriors to end a nine-game losing streak. He nearly repeated the feat in his next game, a 104–94 loss to the Los Angeles Lakers, when he had eleven points, eight assists, and ten rebounds.

Stephen was the only Warrior to stay on the court all season. He started seventy-seven games, thirteen more than the next highest total, Ellis's sixty-four. Among those games Ellis missed was a four-game road trip in April, the final month of the season. Without their leading scorer, the Warriors looked to Stephen to put up points. He averaged a terrific twenty-eight points, 8.5 assists, and 6.5 rebounds per game, as the Warriors went 2–2. On and off the court, Stephen had become a leader to the team's young players, who Coach Nelson began to call "Curry's guys."

In the final game of the season, Stephen gave Golden State fans a preview of the coming decade. He scored forty-two points and shot four of six three-point attempts in a 122–116 comeback win against the Portland Trail Blazers. That performance increased his season averages to 17.5 points and 5.9 assists. After an excellent first year, Stephen was named All-Rookie first team and finished second in Rookie of the Year voting to Tyreke Evans.

Stephen and Monta Ellis were the two bright spots on a Warriors team that went 26–56. Despite his protests about playing with Stephen, Ellis had a career year, averaging 25.5 points per game. Still, a sense remained that Golden State would one day soon have to choose between their two talented young guards.

That off-season, Stephen made the USA team and traveled to Turkey for the FIBA World Championship. Stephen played sparingly coming off the bench, but won a gold medal as the United States went undefeated.

All that winning had to be a nice break for Stephen.

He had more losing ahead of him in his second season on Golden State, despite an eventful off-season for the team. That summer, the franchise got a new owner: Joe Lacob, a businessman. Lacob promised that sometime in the next five years, the Warriors would win their first championship since 1975. He promoted assistant coach Keith Smart to head coach. Golden State also swung a trade to get All-Star big man David Lee from the Knicks. The Warriors even got new jerseys, ditching navy and red for the golden-bridge-against-a-blue-sky logo Stephen would make famous.

Those changes led to modest improvements from the team, which won thirty-six games. Stephen, though, seemed to regress in certain areas. While his scoring improved, he struggled with fouls. Smart often pulled Stephen for a defensive replacement in key situations. Stephen also suffered multiple serious ankle sprains throughout the season, which kept him out of games.

That January, the new Warriors owner acknowledged Stephen's inconsistencies and called Monta Ellis the team's franchise player. Lacob even said he would trade Stephen if he thought it would improve the team. Stephen expressed surprise at his boss's remarks. He played better from that point on, making almost half of his shots for the remainder of the year. He also won the league's Sportsmanship Award that season, as voted on by the players.

Though he didn't trade Curry, Lacob clearly intended to shake up his franchise. After another losing season, he made his second coaching change in as many years. Mark Jackson, a former teammate of Dell Curry, got the job. Someone who had once shot around for fun with a preteen Stephen Curry was now tasked with unleashing his full NBA potential.

Also during the off-season, Stephen underwent surgery on his right ankle. Multiple sprains the season before had caused damage. His doctors expected him to be ready for training camp. With a clean bill of health and new coach, Stephen had reason to be optimistic.

It was the most important summer of twenty-three-year-old Stephen Curry's life, though not because of a new coach, surgery, or expectations going into his third season. On July 31, 2011, Stephen married his girlfriend, Ayesha Alexander. They had met as high schoolers in their church youth group in Charlotte. They had both lived in Toronto as kids and bonded over their favorite Canadian candy. They didn't date, however, until Stephen visited Los Angeles for the ESPYS in college. He reconnected with Ayesha, who was pursuing an acting career. Three years later, they wed in Charlotte. Soon after that, they were expecting their first child. Whatever happened next for Stephen on the court, he was a father now.

# ★ CHAPTER TEN ★

## 2011–2012

### Setbacks and the Trade

A lockout shortened the 2011–2012 NBA season, which didn't start until Christmas Day. The delay seemed to favor Stephen, who got more time to rehabilitate after surgery and adjust to married life. But in the Warriors' final preseason game, while running backward to get on defense, Stephen sprained his right ankle yet again. He left the arena on crutches.

At first, the news on Stephen's injury seemed good. The work of the surgery had not been undone. During just the second game of the season, however, Stephen left early after aggravating the injury. Nine days later, in a game against the San Antonio Spurs, Stephen sprained his ankle again. Just five games into the season, he had suffered the same injury three times. He was understandably frustrated.

Even as he returned to play most of Golden State's February games, Stephen's ankle hurt. The Warriors ultimately shut Stephen down for the final twenty-eight contests of the season. He missed forty games in total. To make matters worse for the Warriors, they had let backup point guard and California native Jeremy Lin go to the Knicks at the beginning of the season. Filling in for injured guards on his new team, Lin emerged as the surprise superstar of that season. "Linsanity" swept the nation.

Stephen's injury sunk the Warriors' playoff chances. They finished the season 23–43, near the bottom of the standings. The situation did at least secure Stephen's place on the team. Since drafting him, Golden State had resisted trading Stephen in many rumored would-be deals for big-name stars. Now his uncertain health greatly reduced his trade value. No team wanted to give up top assets for a player who seemingly couldn't make it through a week without getting hurt.

With Curry out and the team floundering, general manager Larry Riley finally chose between his two undersized guards: the Warriors traded Monta Ellis. Golden State sent the twenty-six-year-old scorer to the Milwaukee Bucks for Andrew Bogut, a seven-foot Australian center, who would give them a much-needed defensive presence on the interior.

On March 19, 2012, six days after the big trade, the Warriors held a ceremony at halftime to honor retired Warriors great Chris Mullin. When owner Joe Lacob took the microphone to speak, the fans booed. In the middle of the team's fifth straight losing season, the Golden State faithful were not happy with the franchise trading its best player. Stephen and Bogut both being injured didn't help the mood.

The Monta Ellis trade actually set the Warriors on a path to success. When Stephen eventually did return, he would no longer have to compete with Ellis for shots. He would be the undisputed offensive engine of the team. Ellis's departure also opened up a spot in the starting lineup for rookie shooting guard Klay Thompson. The Warriors' first-round pick that off-season, Thompson stepped in for Ellis and averaged 18.6 points per game for the rest of the season.

Thompson's dad, Mychal Thompson, had played in the NBA. His mom was a college volleyball player. And Klay arrived from college with a reputation for shooting three-pointers. Sound familiar? Maybe the only thing Thompson and Stephen don't have in common is height. Thompson, three inches taller than his teammate, makes up for Stephen's size in a way Monta Ellis could not.

Given Ellis's public statements three seasons before, the duo of him and Stephen seemed doomed from the start. Thompson and Stephen were about to become a pairing unlike anything the NBA had ever seen.

# ★ CHAPTER ELEVEN ★

## 2012–2013

### Splash Brothers

Stephen Curry rolled his right ankle...again. The Warriors were playing their eleventh game of the 2012–2013 NBA season against the Mavericks in Dallas. Down 78–73 early in the fourth quarter, Stephen drew a foul driving toward the basket. But after landing awkwardly on an opponent, he didn't get up right away to take his free throws. He limped to the line and made both shots. As Dallas tried to get those two points back, Stephen intercepted a pass and dribbled up the floor despite obvious pain. He made a layup to cut the lead to one point. Dallas called a time-out.

Monta Ellis was long gone. Stephen was the team's new leader. So when they came out of the time-out, he enthusiastically took the floor, in spite of his injury. Golden State fans had a right to wonder in those minutes if another lost season was in store. The people who questioned the Warriors' decision before the season to give Stephen a four-year, $44 million contract extension might soon look smart.

But Stephen was focused on neither his ankle nor his season. He wanted to win that game, to give the Warriors a 6–5 winning record. With 6:07 remaining, he rose up right in the face of a defender to hit a jumper, giving the Warriors an 81–80 lead. With three minutes left, he created another shot, going from a crossover dribble to a pump fake in one quick motion. *Swish!* Golden State led by one, as Curry let out a shout to pump up his team. He scored fourteen of his team's last seventeen points in regulation to force overtime.

Then, in overtime, he took over. On their first possession, Stephen drove off a pick to lay a soft floater into the net. Next he found teammate Festus Ezeli on a no-look pass to set up an easy dunk. Stephen pumped his fist in the air as the jam went down. When they got the ball back, Stephen hit rookie forward Harrison Barnes for a wide-open three. He jumped up and down with his arms in the air before Barnes even got the shot off, as if willing it to go down. The Warriors had opened overtime on a 7–0 run, all Stephen's doing. They won the game 105–101.

"Everybody kind of was thinking, 'Here we go again,'" new Golden State general manager Bob Myers told the *Associated Press*. "He kind of had this look—it was like a boxer who takes a punch and starts laughing.

He . . . came out guns blazing and performed exception-ally well and won us the game, really."

Golden State had a winning record, and would for the rest of that season. Stephen did not keep injuring his ankle after that game, as he had in years past. He did, however, keep making shots and plays, and pumping up his teammates.

A few games later, Stephen went on a four-game streak in which he had at least twenty points and ten assists. He owed the point totals to a newfound emphasis on three-pointers. In his first three seasons, Stephen had averaged 4.7 three-pointers attempted per game. That number jumped to 7.7 in year four, with no Monta Ellis around.

Stephen's increase in assists came thanks to his new shooting guard. Klay Thompson attempted 6.4 treys per game himself. Together, he and Stephen became known as the Splash Brothers for their ability to make deep nothing-but-net shots that seem to "splash" the twine. For most players, the sheer volume of threes would mean they were taking more bad shots. But Thompson still managed a 40.1 three-point percentage. Stephen posted an excellent 45.3 percent.

The timing of his three-point barrage couldn't have been better. Before the season, Stephen teamed up with the United Nations Foundation's Nothing But Nets campaign. For every three-pointer hit that season,

Stephen pledged to send three bed nets to families who need them. In countries where mosquitos can carry malaria, those nets save lives. He would end up donating more than eight hundred nets that season alone.

Stephen demonstrated just how many treys he could hit in a February game against the Knicks. He had once wanted New York to draft him so he could put on amazing shooting displays in Madison Square Garden. He ended up doing that anyway.

The Warriors star had a quiet first quarter. He made some nice passes but scored just four points and his team trailed. Then, with nine minutes left in the half, the Knicks defense lost Curry in the corner. With his man arriving late, Stephen made an easy three. A little more than a minute later in the game, he pulled up and drained another deep shot, right in the face of a defender. Now down just four, Thompson and Stephen combined to steal the ball from Knicks superstar Carmelo Anthony. Leading a three-on-two fast break down the court, Stephen looked off both of his teammates, pulled up at the three-point line, and let it fly. *Splash!* He knew he was hot.

With a little more than five minutes left, Stephen tried one a foot behind the line. The ball hit the back of the rim and went in. Golden State had the lead and Stephen had seemingly unlimited range.

In the second half, he hit threes from everywhere:

the corner, the top of the arc (twice), way behind the line, next to the scorer's table, and in front of the Knicks coach (twice). Down 99–97, Stephen hit a trey in transition, despite a defender's hand in his face. The shot was so perfect the net barely moved as the ball passed through. The Knicks fans let out a collective gasp. Stephen danced back down the court, his arms flopping loosey-goosey behind his back. The Baby-Faced Assassin celebrated like a kid. But he was beating adults.

Stephen hit eleven out of thirteen three-pointers—a Golden State record—and scored fifty-four points. Believe it or not, the Warriors lost, 109–105. (Part of the problem was that the point guard outscored the rest of the team 54–51.) Still, Stephen had dominated on one of the NBA's biggest stages in a nationally televised game. His fifty-four points surpassed Kevin Durant's fifty-two for the most scored in a single game that season. He was on the brink of superstardom.

While Stephen never matched fifty-four points again that season, he exploded several more times: he made at least six threes fourteen times. The Warriors were chasing a playoff spot, and Stephen was chasing history. He had a chance to break Ray Allen's record of 269 three-pointers made in a single season.

Golden State achieved the first feat on April 9, 2013, when they clinched a playoff appearance with a 105–89 win over the Minnesota Timberwolves. Eight days later the Warriors played the Trail Blazers in Portland with Stephen at 268 threes. In the first quarter, Stephen came off a screen to hit a wide-open shot to tie Ray Allen's record. Then, midway through the second, he took a pass and hit number 270. With a fist pump and a quick point to the sky, Stephen acknowledged the historic importance of the moment. He finished the game with 272 threes.

Golden State entered the playoffs as the Western Conference's sixth seed and drew third-seed Denver. The Nuggets had lost just three times in Denver all season, making their home court advantage seem especially ominous for the Warriors. Stephen, however, knew all about winning big games as an underdog.

The series started as expected, with Denver taking Game 1 at home, 97–95. The Nuggets excelled at frustrating Stephen, who made just seven shots. Even worse, Golden State power forward David Lee injured his hip during the game. An All-Star and the team's second-leading scorer after Stephen, Lee missed the rest of the playoffs.

Game 2 started similarly with the two teams trading blows. Then Stephen started finding teammates. With two minutes left in the first quarter, he threw the ball across his chest with his off hand to backup guard Jarrett Jack, who got to the rim with a floater. At the beginning of the second, Stephen drove to the hoop.

When the defense collapsed to stop him, he heaved a one-handed pass to find Draymond Green across the floor, wide open for a three. After the Nuggets answered on their next possession, Stephen drew four defenders with another convincing drive before again finding a teammate wide open for a trey. Then, as Denver finally started to respect the pass, he showed them the shot.

Halfway through the second, Stephen got the ball, pump-faked, crossed over his defender, and finally made a jumper while falling into his own team's bench. The Warriors took a 47–42 lead, and it only grew from there. In addition to his thirteen assists, Stephen scored thirty points. Thompson added twenty-one of his own on just eleven shots—he made five shots from three. Golden State won, 131–117.

"In my opinion, they're the greatest shooting backcourt in the history of the game," Coach Mark Jackson said about the Splash Brothers afterward.

Jackson's statement caused a stir. But his two young stars backed it up. Stephen posted another double-double—twenty-nine points and eleven assists—in the next game, the first NBA playoff game in Oakland in six years. And after winning both home games and losing once more in Denver, the Warriors returned to Oracle Arena for Game 6 with a chance to complete the upset. Denver kept Stephen under wraps early. Then, just as he had done time after time in the NCAA Tournament, Stephen turned a first-half deficit into a second-half comeback as he exploded for fourteen points on four three-pointers.

"I pulled [Stephen] aside and told him, 'There's going to be a point in this game when you take over, because you're the best player on the floor,'" Coach Jackson said. "Sure enough, that's exactly what took place."

Jackson had a point: as talented as the Nuggets were, they didn't have a star like Stephen Curry. In the second round, facing the San Antonio Spurs, the Warriors wouldn't have that advantage. Tim Duncan had already won four titles and looked poised to claim another after a fifty-eight-win regular season.

It turned out the mighty Spurs were immune to the Stephen Curry second-half explosion. Game 1, in San Antonio, started with the Warriors grabbing a modest 53–49 despite a slow start from Stephen. Ninety seconds into the second half, Stephen made a shot that suggested he was suddenly on. Covered by two Spurs, he stepped back and hit a long two in the corner while falling backward. He ended up sitting in a front-row seat; the ball ended up in the hoop.

A minute later he hit a three in the face of Tony Parker, a future Hall of Famer. Whenever a Spur defender went to help out on Stephen, the Warriors point guard immediately found the open man. With

2:48 left in the third quarter, Stephen dribbled up to Parker again, going through his legs, then behind his back. He then accidentally dropped the ball, bent down to pick it up, and popped up to nail a shot from just inside the arc. His teammates on the Golden State bench jokingly stood up with distressed looks on their faces and their hands on their heads. The things their friend was doing to those poor Spurs!

Possession after possession that quarter, Stephen made shots. He punctuated the run by hitting a three-pointer while nearly standing on the S in the Spurs' half-court logo. The San Antonio crowd groaned. The Golden State bench exploded. The Warriors led 90–72. Stephen had scored twenty-two points in the quarter.

Then the Spurs proved what made them different from any other playoff team Stephen had ever faced: they came back. Slowly but surely they climbed out of that eighteen-point hole, forced overtime, and won.

The Warriors won two games in the series. But the Game 1 double-overtime loss loomed large as they dropped three more games by double digits and lost the series. Regardless, Stephen and Golden State had come far. Before the season, a winning record was no sure bet for the Warriors, and many doubted Stephen's ability to stay on the court. Next season, fans and management would expect more.

# ★ CHAPTER TWELVE ★

## 2013–2014

## All-Star

Stephen proved that his 2012–2013 season was no flash in the pan. He returned next season even better, increasing his points per game (twenty-four) and assists per game (8.5, still a career high). The Warriors improved as a team, too, mainly on defense. That off-season they added forward Andre Iguodala, the best player on the Nuggets team they had beaten in the first round of the playoffs. Rangy and athletic, the six-foot-six Iguodala had a reputation for shutting down opponents' best players.

Still, the Warriors struggled to establish themselves among the top teams in the West, like the Spurs. Golden State went 0–4 against San Antonio during the regular season. The Warriors seemed destined for the playoffs, but could they take the next step?

Individually, Stephen earned recognition as one of the league's best players. In January, fans voted him to his first ever All-Star team. A starter for the West,

Stephen was one of just four players to receive over a million votes. Stephen's peers also recognized how good he had become. Kevin Durant tweeted that Stephen was the "best shooter to ever play."

"I grew up watching my dad in the NBA," Stephen said. "Every February, we watched the All-Star Game. I've been to a few as a kid, when my dad was in the three-point contest. I understand how big a deal it is to be selected."

Stephen starred off the court, too. That off-season, he helped hand out thirty-eight thousand bed nets in Tanzania as part of Nothing But Nets. Around Christmas, Stephen bought food for four hundred families in Oakland. He also helped deserving kids through camps, clinics, and the Make-A-Wish Foundation. After the season, he would win the Seasonlong Kia Community Assist Award, which came with a $25,000 contribution to the charity of Stephen's choosing.

"I love helping out," Stephen told a reporter. "There is no better feeling than doing something for others. It's a great thrill just to be able to assist in any way I can."

The Warriors finished the regular season 51–31, making them the sixth seed in the Western Conference again. That year, the third seed was the LA Clippers, a tougher opponent than the Nuggets the year before. Led by their giant frontcourt duo of Blake Griffin and DeAndre Jordan, the Clippers gained a reputation for powerful dunks. Lob City—named for their ability to slam down alley-oops from point guard Chris Paul—contrasted the Splash Brothers' long-distance shooting.

Early in the series, it seemed as if LA's strength would win out. With their own paint protector, Andrew Bogut, out for the series, Golden State struggled to stop Griffin and Jordan. With the series tied 2–2, Jordan scored twenty-five points and added eighteen rebounds in Game 5, and the Clippers won easily, 113–103. The Warriors needed to win two games to keep their season alive.

In Game 6, Stephen and Klay shot poorly, making twelve shots combined. Stephen proved he could find other ways to win, however, setting up teammates all night to earn nine assists and the 100–99 win. That trend continued in Game 7. When the Clippers tried to double-team Stephen early, he found power forward Draymond Green, who hit three quick three-pointers and would finish with twenty-four points. Other times, Stephen shot over the heads of the double-team. With ten seconds left in the half, he did just that, getting a three and the foul. Bombing away from deep, Golden State took a 64–56 lead into the locker room.

The Clippers came out at halftime, however, and went on a 12–2 run to grab the lead. In the fourth quarter, the Warriors were again unable to stop DeAndre Jordan and Blake Griffin. Jordan dunked to give the

Clippers a 108–107 lead, then blocked a Stephen layup, leading to a Griffin alley-oop slam the other way. Those two kept punishing the Warriors en route to a 126–121 win.

"We fought so hard this whole series, this whole season," Stephen said. "It stings."

Suddenly, there seemed to be no guarantee that Mark Jackson would return as head coach next season. The Warriors had turned their franchise around under his watch, going from constant losing seasons to back-to-back playoff appearances. The loss to the Clippers had been disappointing but hardly seemed like grounds for firing the coach. Stephen and Jackson were close, and the point guard defended his coach.

"I love Coach more than anybody, and I think for him to be in a situation where his job is under scrutiny and under question is totally unfair," Stephen said. "And it would definitely be a shock to me if anything like that were to happen."

Stephen's teammates agreed with him. But Jackson's relationship with management had become strained. On May 6, 2014, the Warriors fired their coach. Steve Kerr, the former three-point specialist on Michael Jordan's Chicago Bulls, became Stephen's fourth boss in six years. Stephen may not have liked Jackson's dismissal, but he would love life under Kerr.

# ★ CHAPTER THIRTEEN ★

## 2014–2015

## The Dream Season

The Warriors got a rematch with the Clippers for their fourth game of the 2014–2015 season. Despite these two teams having played each other just six months ago with basically the exact same rosters, this time it wasn't close. Golden State led by as much as twenty-nine points at certain points in the game. They won 121–104 and improved to 4–0 on the season, their best start in twenty years.

After the game, owner Joe Lacob visited the Warriors dressing room to celebrate. He shook Stephen's hand and asked a question.

"That's what we envisioned, right?"

What Steve Kerr had envisioned was an exciting new offense for his team. Under Mark Jackson, the Warriors had played a lot of ISO basketball, meaning plays in which one player tried to beat his man while his teammates got out of the way. Kerr's style demanded speed, motion, and constant passing. The season before,

Golden State had been last in the league in passes per possession. In 2014–2015, they learned to share the rock.

This new style suited Stephen, who could play more off the ball, running around the floor to get open. It also allowed him to show off his creative passing skills. Ten games into the season, the Warriors played the Lakers. Stephen finished with thirty points and fifteen assists. Early in the game, seeing Stephen's assist total on the scoreboard, Kerr turned to one of his assistants and asked, "Is that right?" Kobe Bryant scored forty-four points in that game, but the Warriors won easily, 136–115. After the game, Klay Thompson declared his team title contenders. Stephen agreed, but stressed they needed to "stay humble" with lots of games left on the schedule. Then Coach Kerr made a pronouncement of his own.

"That's as good a job at point guard as I've ever seen, what Steph did tonight—managing the game, being aggressive at the right times, taking care of the ball and finding guys," Kerr said. "The guy has taken it to another level. I think he's the best in the NBA right now at that position."

As the season went on, few could argue that Stephen was the best at his position. Not only was he shooting and passing as well as ever, other aspects of his game had progressed, including his defense. No Warriors coach had ever fully trusted Stephen to hold his own at the other end of the floor. Even Mark Jackson had assigned Klay Thompson to cover the toughest opposing point guards. But Kerr trusted Stephen to play aggressively. The move paid off: Stephen paced the NBA with 163 steals that season.

Nine days after blowing out the Lakers, Golden State went to Miami, where the Heat got off to an early fifteen-point lead. Stephen put all his skills on display that night to bring his team out of that hole. In one second-quarter sequence, he grabbed the rebound on defense and brought it up the court. When Miami met him with a double-team, he dribbled behind his back, through his legs, and then again behind his back to get open and drain a three.

He would make eight threes in that game, giving him forty points for the night. And when the Heat tried to double-team him, he simply found open teammates, which netted him seven assists. And through all that, he turned the ball over only twice. The Warriors came all the way back, not just to win, but to win easily, 114–97. Kerr said Stephen had played "the perfect game."

Turnovers had been a problem for Stephen in the past. The season before, he had been one away from tying the league lead. The best players in the NBA usually have the most turnovers because they do the most with the ball. But Stephen resolved to improve with help from his mom, Sonya. They made a bet: Stephen would have to pay his mom for every turnover he made in excess of three a game. He could make money back by having fewer than three in a game.

Fans noticed how hard Stephen had worked to improve his game. His improved handle, which let him dribble through defenders, and his ability to get hot from behind the arc combined to make him a human highlight reel. He made passes without looking and banked amazing shots high off the glass. That season, fans didn't just vote him to the All-Star team: they voted for him more than any other player, including LeBron James. The Warriors were on top of the standings, and Stephen was the biggest reason why.

Even when Golden State played poorly, Stephen had the ability to pull out the win. Less than seven minutes into a game against the Dallas Mavericks in February, the Warriors found themselves down 24–4! But Stephen made a series of seemingly impossible shots and drives to bring his team all the way back. Then, with the Warriors leading by three points in the third quarter, Stephen really got hot. He hit threes from all areas and at all distances. With the game tied 88–88, Stephen stepped into his defender, dribbled the ball back and forth between his legs, then stepped back to shoot well behind the line. *Swish!* Coach Steve Kerr closed his eyes and shook his head, as if even he couldn't believe it.

With less than a minute left in the game, Stephen had forty-eight points on nine three-pointers made. Draymond Green told him, "Get fifty." So Stephen tried one more shot from way back. *Bang!* The crowd erupted. He finished with fifty-one points, and the Warriors won 128–114.

"Sometimes Steph plays his best when we're down big, and he just senses that he has to put the Superman cape on," Kerr said. "And he's so good at it. He loves the freedom of being down and saying, 'All right. I'm going to let it fly and bring us back.' And that's what he did."

Stephen was Superman for Golden State all season, as they won a franchise record sixty-seven games and clinched the first seed in the West. Stephen broke his own three-point record with 286 makes.

His team's success combined with his incredible plays and humble personality made Stephen the NBA's biggest star. He appeared in commercials and signed endorsement deals, and his jersey started popping up everywhere. He also became a frontrunner to win Most Valuable Player at the end of the season. Stephen wasn't focused on any individual awards, however. This season, the Warriors wanted to win the championship.

# ★ CHAPTER FOURTEEN ★

## 2015

### MVP and Champion

The Warriors didn't need to win Game 3 of their first-round series against the New Orleans Pelicans. They already had a 2–0 lead in the series after winning the first two games at home. Still, Golden State couldn't feel good about being down 101–84 in the fourth quarter to the eighth seed, a team they were supposed to crush. For all the expectation from their regular season success, Golden State still remembered the first round the year before.

Still down ten points with 2:50 remaining, Klay Thompson made a turnaround jumper to cut the lead to eight. The New Orleans fans murmured. Their team was probably okay. Thirty-five seconds later, Stephen Curry missed a shot—a good sign for the Pelicans. But Draymond Green put back the rebound. The lead was just six. Then Green did it again. Four-point game.

After several misses from the Warriors and free

throws from each team, the Pelicans seemed to have the game back in hand, 107–102. With seventeen seconds left, the Warriors would get the ball, but they couldn't get five points on one possession. Green kicked the ball to Stephen on the point. He pump-faked, letting his defender fly past him, then drained a three. With 11.8 seconds on the clock, the lead was just two.

Golden State fouled to stop the clock, and Pelicans star Anthony Davis made one of two free throws. With ten seconds left, the Warriors would get the ball back, down by three. They inbounded the ball to Stephen. With a defender right up in his face, Stephen made a desperate heave toward the basket, while falling backward. *Clank!* The ball glanced off the rim. But like so many other high-arcing, butter-soft Steph Curry shots, the rebound was manageable and fielded by Warriors big man Marreese Speights. Curry bolted toward the left corner. Speights pitched the ball to Stephen who immediately put it up before being tackled by a desperate Davis. *Splash!* Tie game. Overtime.

In overtime, Stephen picked up right where he left off, hitting an immediate three, and the Warriors never looked back. They won, 123–119, taking a three-game lead and demoralizing the Pelicans in the process. Two days later, the Warriors completed the sweep with an eleven-point victory on the road.

The next round started well, too, with the Warriors

easily defeating the Grizzlies in Game 1. The next day, on May 4, 2015, the league announced the winner of the 2014–2015 MVP Award. Stephen Curry won basketball's highest individual honor.

"First and foremost, I have to thank my Lord and Savior Jesus Christ for blessing me with the talents to play this game, with a family that supports me day in and day out," Stephen said when he took the podium for his acceptance speech. "I'm His humble servant right now."

With his family sitting in the front row, Stephen began to recount his story, thanking the important people in his life. First, he thanked Ayesha, his "backbone," recalling how they met as kids. He referenced their now two-year-old daughter, Riley, who was sitting in her grandmother Sonya's lap, and Riley's little sister, who was still on the way.

Then he thanked his parents, starting with his mom. He expressed appreciation for how she had disciplined him and his siblings, and taught them priorities.

"That's a pretty embarrassing moment if you go to your first middle school game and you have to tell your team, 'Hey fellas, I can't play tonight; I didn't do the dishes at home,'" Stephen said. The audience laughed.

Stephen then turned to his father: "I remember a lot of your career. And to be able to follow in your footsteps..." He became choked up and put his head down

71

for a moment, before finishing: "It means a lot to me." Dell welled up with tears.

The list of people Stephen wanted to thank was long, and he took time for all of them: his brother and sister, his grandmother, Coach Kerr, Coach McKillop, and the fans, among many others. Before finally thanking each teammate individually, Stephen summed up his entire life as "the ultimate paradox":

"I'm the son of a sixteen-year NBA veteran....I was blessed to have a family that never really struggled when I was growing up thanks to my dad and his career. We had the means to do a lot growing up. You would think that my future was set based on that fact, and that couldn't be farther from the truth.

"I was always the smallest kid on my team. I had a terrible, ugly, catapult shot from the time I was four-teen because I wasn't strong enough to shoot over my head. And I had to reconstruct that over the summer, and it was the worst three months of my life. You'd think there are no hurdles or obstacles that I had to overcome, but even when I got to high school, I wasn't ranked. I wasn't ranked. I wasn't highly touted as a high school prospect. I had nobody really running, knocking on my door saying, 'Please, please, please come play for our school,' until Coach McKillop called.

"Everything happens for a reason, and there is a story to everything. If you take time to realize what your dream is and what you really want in life—no matter what it is, whether it's sports or in other fields— you have to realize that there is always work to do, and you want to be the hardest-working person in whatever you do, and you put yourself in a position to be successful. And you have to have a passion about what you do. Basketball was mine, and that's what's carried me to this point."

It was a great recounting of his story. There was only one problem: his story wasn't finished yet. The next day, Stephen had to play the Grizzlies and shot uncharacteristically poorly. The next game, in Memphis, Stephen struggled again, hitting just two threes. Down 1–2 in their second-round series, the Warriors would have to fight to keep their dream season alive.

"Steph has a big burden on his shoulders," Warriors coach Steve Kerr said. "He's the MVP of the league, and their defensive focus is on him. We've got to do a better job of helping free him up, and he's got to do a better job of trusting his teammates."

Still, the Warriors didn't want to change too much. Stephen could stay cold for only so long. And sure enough, for the next three games of the series, Stephen shot 51.4 percent from behind the arc and averaged 27.7 points. The Warriors won all three by double digits. For the first time in his career, Stephen would play in the Western Conference finals.

To play in the NBA Finals, the Warriors had to beat the Houston Rockets, led by James Harden, the MVP runner-up. The Rockets also boasted center Dwight Howard, one of the most powerful big men in the game. In the previous year's playoffs, the Warriors had not been able to handle another punishing center, DeAndre Jordan, with Andrew Bogut hurt.

In Game 1 in Oakland, the Rockets came out stronger than the Warriors, leading 51–37 halfway through the second quarter. Not wanting a repeat of last year, Kerr countered Howard by doing something risky: he took Bogut out. Rather than try to match Houston's size inside, the Warriors went small, playing six-foot-seven Draymond Green at center and surrounding him with shooters. With a lineup of five shorter players who could all hit threes, Golden State could play faster and create a mismatch. It worked: the Warriors' new lineup went on a 21–4 run before halftime to grab a three-point lead. They would hang on and win by four points, 110–106.

Game 1 also produced a brand-new superstar: Stephen's daughter, Riley. During her dad's postgame press conference, Riley appeared and demanded to sit in his lap. When Stephen started his first answer about battling Harden with "It's entertaining basketball..." Riley started laughing. When Stephen shushed her, she replied, "Be quiet." Riley waved at the reporters, coughed, and fake-sneezed.

"Are you in control of her at home?" one reporter asked.

"She is just like this. She's only two—it's the craziest thing ever," Stephen replied. Riley's antics made her nearly as popular online as her dad.

In Game 2, it was the Warriors who almost blew the lead. Up 98–90 with 1:39 left in the game, Harden scored six quick points before setting up Dwight Howard for an alley-oop slam. The Warriors made just one free throw in that span and led 99–98 with thirty-three seconds left. Golden State ran down the clock and then, with the shot clock expiring, forward Harrison Barnes missed a reverse layup. Harden grabbed the rebound and drove up the court with just eight seconds left. This time, however, it would be the Splash Brothers' defense that saved the day, as they double-teamed Harden and forced him to lose the ball as the buzzer sounded.

Behind a signature forty-point performance from Stephen, the Warriors won Game 3 in Houston 115–80 en route to a 4–1 series win. No team in the Western Conference had seriously challenged the Golden State Warriors. They were headed to the NBA Finals.

Waiting for them were the Cleveland Cavaliers and

LeBron James. Seven years ago, LeBron, already an NBA star, had flown just to watch little Stephen Curry lead Davidson to a surprising March Madness run. Now, in his first season back in Cleveland, he hoped to end Stephen's similarly amazing NBA playoff run. The Cavaliers were without forward Kevin Love, one third of the Cavs' "Big Three" along with LeBron and Kyrie Irving. Still, no team led by LeBron would roll over. Stephen may have been MVP, but LeBron had already won the award four times.

In Game 1 in Oakland, LeBron gave an MVP-level performance. He took on a cast of Warriors defenders and beat them all. He would finish the game with forty-four points. Golden State, meanwhile, got the whole team involved in the offense. Five Warriors logged double-digit points. The result was an even game that ended 98–98 in regulation.

The overtime period, however, was lopsided. Stephen got fouled twice and made all four shots. The Cavaliers didn't score until a LeBron layup with time expiring. Golden State prevailed, 108–100.

In Game 2, the Cavaliers would be without Kyrie Irving, leaving LeBron as the team's only remaining star. He accepted the challenge, however, playing in the low post, slowing the game down, and physically dominating. LeBron finished the game with a triple-double:

thirty-nine points, sixteen rebounds, and eleven assists. Stephen had his worst shooting performance of the season, making just five of twenty-three attempts.

Still, the Warriors got within striking distance. And with eleven seconds left, down 87–85, they got the ball to Stephen. He lost LeBron off a pick and crossed over the defender who switched onto him, going to the hoop for the easy layin. For the second game in a row, there would be overtime. This time, however, the Cavs defended too well. The Finals headed back to Cleveland tied.

Stephen played better in Game 3. But the rest of Golden State's starters struggled, and LeBron remained a one-man team, scoring forty points, grabbing twelve rebounds, and dishing out eight assists. The Warriors lost 96–91 and, for the second time that postseason, found themselves in a 2–1 hole. The solution was the same: keep shooting. The Warriors made 46.8 percent of their shots in Game 4 and 48 percent in Game 5, winning both easily. As they had against Houston, Golden State found success going small against a bigger opponent. The series returned to Cleveland with the Warriors on the cusp of a title.

The teams traded lopsided quarters in the first half. The Warriors, led by Stephen, were up 28–15 after the first. Then the Cavaliers got within two points going into halftime, largely thanks to the interior defense of Timofey Mozgov. There would be no three-point flurry from Stephen in the final twenty-four minutes, but he made his shots count. The Cavaliers went on a 7–0 run early in the fourth quarter, punctuated by a LeBron steal and dunk. Down just 75–68, Cleveland seemed to have the moment, feeding off the energy of their home crowd. But Stephen quieted the fans with a step-back three that put the lead back in double digits. When the Cavs again got close, cutting the lead to 83–75, the MVP scored once more from deep.

Late in the fourth quarter, the Cavaliers made a desperate final bid. Cleveland's J. R. Smith made a Stephen Curry–esque three to bring his team within four. On the next possession, however, Stephen went to the line and calmly sunk two free throws to ice the game. With ten seconds left on the clock and his team losing 104–97, LeBron walked over to Stephen and shook his hand. It was over. For the first time since 1975, the Golden State Warriors were NBA champions.

Ayesha, Dell, Sonya, Sydel, and Riley came onto the floor, jumping and screaming, to congratulate Stephen. Then he and Riley climbed onstage to claim the Larry O'Brien NBA Championship Trophy.

"This is what it's all about," Stephen said. "To have our families here, our whole team, coaching staff—everybody be a part of it...we're going to remember this for a long time."

Six years after getting drafted by the wrong team, four years after having his career derailed by an injury, and one year after getting bounced in the first round, Stephen Curry was on top.

# ★ CHAPTER FIFTEEN ★

## 2015–2016

## The Best Ever?

A season after winning the MVP Award and the championship, what could Stephen Curry possibly do as a follow-up? Get a lot better, it turns out. As more days passed, it became clear that something special was happening. Through his first three games, Stephen scored 118 points in ninety-nine minutes on sixty-eight shots. After his fourth game, he already had three twenty-point quarters. That was three times the number any other player in the NBA had!

Stephen was shooting more often and farther from the basket. Yet even as his job got more difficult, he became *more* accurate. During his 2014–2015 MVP campaign, Stephen had attempted 653 shots and made 48.7 percent. In 2015–2016, he would throw up 805 and make more than half. After twenty-four games, he averaged over five three-pointers made per game, putting him on pace to shatter his own single-season record.

The Warriors went 24–0 in those games, the best start in NBA history. (They annihilated the previous record of 15–0.) Stephen had gained recognition as the greatest shooter in NBA history. So why not have him fire away?

Stephen could shoot and shoot and his aim never seemed to suffer. The season before, he had twenty-three games with double-digit three-point attempts. In 2015–2016, he took at least ten shots behind the arc in fifty-three different contests. And the number would have been even higher had he not sat out eighteen fourth quarters when the Warriors already had the game practically won! The player who been knocked his whole career for not being a typical point guard was remaking the game in his image. The three-point shot ruled the NBA now, and nobody did it better than Stephen.

Even in pregame warm-ups he dazzled. Fans came early to watch him practice, during which he would throw the ball up from all over the floor. On the way back to the locker room, he would make shots standing in the tunnel.

Soon the question became not whether the Warriors would defend their title but whether they were the greatest team ever. The 1995–1996 Bulls, led by Michael Jordan, had gone 72–10 en route to a championship. Golden State had a chance to top that.

The Warriors were so good they were boring. Only nine of their eighty-two games were decided by three points or fewer. Too often Stephen started a game, bombed away, and then rested once it became a blowout. Stephen still had his Superman cape ready, however, in case he ever needed to save his team.

On February 27, 2016, in a Saturday night prime-time game against the Thunder in Oklahoma City, the Warriors found themselves down early thanks to the hot shooting of Kevin Durant. Then, in the second quarter, Stephen erased the deficit in his familiar way: knocking down three triples in quick succession. On the last one, he stood still and held the ball with a defender in a ready defensive stance. Stephen was so far from the top of the arc he was almost out of bounds. But Stephen jumped up anyway to make the shot in the face of the D.

Early in the third, Curry picked off a pass from Durant intended for Russell Westbrook. As he raced the other way for the layup, however, Westbrook bowled him over, knocking him into the base of the basket. An uncharacteristically angry Stephen lay injured under the hoop, yelling at the refs that he had been fouled.

Stephen's old foe, the injured ankle, kept him out of the game for a while. That only made it more impressive when he came back in and started making bucket after bucket after bucket. With 3:39 left on the clock and his team trailing 96–87, Curry went hard to the rim to make a layup. Then he came off a pick to make a shot from well behind the line. 96–92. The teams would trade points to make it 98–93 before Stephen pulled up again from even farther back. Russell Westbrook had given Stephen a little room, thinking not even he could score from that distance. *Bang!* 98–96.

The Thunder scored to make it 100–96. As Curry drove to answer, he got called for traveling, which was rare for him. He laughed, not believing the referees' decision. The Thunder couldn't capitalize on the turnover, though. And when the defense collapsed to stop a streaking Stephen on the next possession, he threw the ball out to Thompson, wide open in the corner for a splash, and they won, 100–99.

Kevin Durant hit a three for what seemed like the dagger, giving Oklahoma a 103–99 lead with just 14.5 seconds to play. After fifty-eight games, it seemed as though the Warriors would finally lose just their sixth contest of the season. Thompson scored a layup, then intercepted a Thunder pass with help from a spectacular Draymond Green keep-in. Andre Iguodala took the final shot. The ball went up. The buzzer sounded. But wait! Durant had fouled Iguodala. He went to the line and made both shots despite a boisterous Oklahoma City crowd. This exciting game was headed to overtime.

The overtime was back and forth. Stephen kept

bombing away and now had eleven three-pointers, one short of the NBA record, despite missing time with his ankle injury. Tied at 118–118 with eleven seconds left in the first overtime period, Westbrook drove to the Warriors net for the win. His fade-away jumper hit off the rim. Andre Iguodala grabbed the rebound and got it to Stephen, who dribbled it up the court with five seconds left.

The Warriors had a time-out, which everyone expected them to take so they could draw up a play. But with three seconds left, Stephen stopped his casual dribble and did something seemingly insane, pulling up to shoot from half-court. No Thunder player was ready to close out on him, because they would never expect a player to attempt a shot thirty feet from the basket, especially not with the game on the line.

*BANG!*

The Warriors on the bench lost their minds. The Thunder players stood, stunned at what they had just witnessed. Even the typically composed Stephen Curry went nuts, jumping up and down, screaming, fist pumping, and finally giving the crowd a shoulder-shake dance. Stephen had won the game, clinched a playoff berth, and tied the single-game three-point record, all with one of the most unbelievable shots ever.

"It's hard to put into words what Steph did," Klay

Thompson said. "It's the most amazing thing I've probably ever seen."

Golden State stayed amazing all season. With one game left in the season and nine losses, the Warriors stared down history. In game eighty-two against the Memphis Grizzlies, Stephen needed less than thirty minutes on the court to drop forty-six points and ten treys. After three quarters, it was obvious that the Warriors had broken the 1995–1996 Bulls' record. So during the fourth quarter, Stephen rested for the playoffs.

After the regular season, Stephen Curry led the league in points per game (30.1) and steals per game (2.1). He had hit 402 three-pointers, obliterating his old record of 286. And he joined the 50-40-90 club, with 50.4 percent shooting from the field, 45.4 percent behind the arc, and 90.8 percent from the free-throw line. Stephen Curry became the only unanimous MVP in NBA history. He now had to be considered among the greatest to ever play the game. And if his team won the championship that season, they could surely claim to be the best ever.

# ⋆ CHAPTER SIXTEEN ⋆

## 2016

### Injuries and Disappointment

For the first two rounds of the 2016 NBA playoffs, the Warriors didn't really have Stephen Curry. Amazingly, they didn't need him. Stephen tweaked his ever-troublesome ankle getting back on defense during Game 1 of their first-round series against the Rockets. He then slipped and sprained his knee during an attempted return in Game 4. Golden State beat Houston in five games, despite Stephen playing just under thirty-eight minutes for the entire series. The Rockets won a single game by one point. The Warriors blew them out by an average of twenty-four points in the other four.

Dealing with the ankle and knee injuries, Stephen sat out the first three games of his team's second-round matchup with Portland. With the Warriors up 2–1, Stephen returned in Games 4 and 5 to score sixty-nine points and send Golden State to the conference finals for the second straight season.

There, the Warriors would face the Thunder, the team on the other end of Stephen's overtime heroics in February. After losing just twice at home all season, Golden State dropped Game 1 at Oracle Arena, 108–102. Kevin Durant and Russell Westbrook flipped the script on Thompson and Stephen, leading an epic second-half comeback. Stephen, despite being banged up, had a double-double with a team-leading twenty-six points and ten rebounds.

The Warriors answered with a resounding 118–91 victory in Game 2, but in the process gave fans a new reason to worry. Jumping in the second row of the crowd to save a loose ball, Stephen had a rough landing. He stayed in the game, but his elbow swelled to the size of a tennis ball.

When the series returned to Oklahoma City, the Thunder struck back, winning 133–105 in Game 3 and 118–94 in Game 4. Stephen shot poorly, making just 23.7 percent from behind the arc. Durant and Westbrook, meanwhile, had two of their best games. The Thunder matched the Warriors' small lineup and, with Stephen not himself, beat the Warriors at their own game.

Usually, losing two basketball games in a row is not a big deal. In this case, it put a team supposedly destined for a championship on the brink of elimination. And for a Warriors squad that hadn't lost two games in a row all season, it signaled something was wrong.

"I think we're a special team, and this isn't how we're going to go out," Stephen said after Game 4.

He stayed true to his word. The Splash Brothers had fifty-eight points in a 120–111 Game 5 win. Then, in Oklahoma City for Game 6, they did even better, combining for seventy-two points and seventeen three-pointers. The biggest shot of the game, however, went for just two. With thirty-seven seconds left in the fourth quarter and the Warriors up 104–101, the Thunder turned the ball over. Stephen took possession with a chance to kill some time. Then, with eighteen seconds left in the game and the shot clock expiring, he crossed over his man, dribbled to the hoop, and softly banked the ball off the top of the glass and in. Stephen looked like himself. The Warriors again seemed like the team of destiny.

Game 7 back at Oracle Arena was a vintage Stephen performance: thirty-six points, seven threes, and eight assists. His teammates didn't shoot well, but it hardly mattered. The Warriors outscored the Thunder by eighteen with Stephen on the floor and won 96–88.

Four more wins and the Warriors would claim the mantle of "greatest team ever." Stephen's all-time great season would be complete. All that remained was a Finals rematch with the Cleveland Cavaliers.

The Cavs returned this year stronger, with Kevin Love and Kyrie Irving healthy and ready to assist

LeBron James. But it didn't seem to matter. In Game 1 in Oakland, the Splash Brothers were cold, but the rest of the team shot well. The Cavaliers, meanwhile, had little offense, managing just 89 points to the Warriors' 104. The score was even more lopsided in Game 2. Despite a back-and-forth start and Stephen playing less than twenty-five minutes due to foul trouble, the Warriors ran away with it, 110–77.

The Cavaliers returned the favor with an equally lopsided victory at home in Game 3, 120–90. But Stephen made sure the Cavs didn't grab the momentum. Two nights later, he scored thirty-eight points in his best game of the playoffs. They were on the brink of back-to-back titles. No team had ever been down 3–1 in the Finals and still come out on top. How would the Cavs do it against the best regular season team ever?

Still, Golden State wanted to end the series in Game 5. If the Cavaliers won, they got to return home, where they had already demonstrated an ability to beat the Warriors. Game 7, if necessary, would be in Oakland. But at that point, anything could happen.

Draymond Green had been suspended for the game for accruing too many flagrant fouls. The loss of their best defensive player didn't seem insurmountable for Golden State after the first half, which was tied 61–61. But for the final twenty-four minutes, LeBron James and Kyrie Irving ran away with the game, scoring forty-one total points each. The series was headed back to Cleveland.

There, Golden State's defense faltered again. Stephen led his team with thirty points, but LeBron, matched up against an injured Andre Iguodala, answered with forty-one points, eleven assists, and eight rebounds. It would all come down to Game 7.

After being suspended for Game 5 and ineffective in Game 6, Draymond Green made up for it with the game of his life. He scored inside and out, hitting six of eight threes and eleven of fifteen shots overall. He ate a ton of glass and found his teammates, too, grabbing fifteen rebounds and dishing out nine assists. For much of the game, that performance was enough for the Warriors. Behind Green, they outshot the Cavaliers from three 10–1 in the first half. A strong third quarter from the Cavaliers, though, brought the game within one point, 76–75, entering the final quarter of the NBA season.

With seven minutes left and his team down three, Stephen crossed over his man and hit a three from well behind the line. The crowd erupted, expecting a familiar scoring explosion from their star point guard to seal the game. But another three never came, as Stephen's next four shots all missed.

That set up an exciting, low-scoring finish. Tied 89–89 for more than two minutes, Stephen and Andre

Iguodala sprung a two-on-one fast break. Stephen sent a perfect bounce pass to Iguodala, who went up for the rebound. But seemingly out of nowhere, LeBron sprinted down the court and blocked the shot against the backboard.

That set up a one-on-one matchup between Kyrie Irving and Stephen on the other end of the court with less than a minute left. Like Stephen had done so many times, Irving created a deep shot off his dribble, shimmying his shoulders to throw Stephen off. Cavs led 92–89.

LeBron would make a free throw, and Stephen would miss his final shot with the clock expiring. Cleveland had its first championship in sixty-four years. The Warriors had completed a stunning series collapse.

"It will haunt me for a while," Stephen said.

# ★ CHAPTER SEVENTEEN ★

## 2017 AND BEYOND

### Just Getting Started

Losing the championship to the Cavaliers was not the final chapter in young Stephen Curry's career. For one thing, it opened the door for the Warriors to improve off-season by adding Kevin Durant. The two top freshman scorers during the 2006–2007 college season and combined back-to-back-to-back NBA MVPs, Durant and Stephen have paired up to form the most talented shooting duo of all time. When Durant signed on with Golden State, he cited all the fun the Warriors seemed to have together. That fun culture didn't exist when Stephen joined the team, and he had as much to do with creating it as anyone.

Stephen's star continues to rise. His shooting in 2015–2016 was the best ever for a single season. That level of play, combined with his selfless attitude, has made Stephen one of the game's most beloved figures. From his humorous Connect Four game against President Obama in an official White House video to his role as designated eater on his wife's cooking show, fans can't get enough of Stephen's off-the-court life and adorable family.

No matter how many MVP Awards or NBA titles he wins, Stephen's journey will always inspire. From the kid at basketball camp who couldn't shoot at all to the greatest shooter in history, Stephen has proved the value of persistence and hard work.

Stephen scrambles for a loose ball in the game against Gonzaga in the 2008 NCAA Men's Basketball Tournament.

During the 2008 NCAA Tournament, Davidson played Georgetown—the favorite to win the game—and Stephen's incredible 25 points in the second half led Davidson to victory.

Up for the shot! Another player tries to block Stephen, but Stephen passes him and leaps for the net.

Ned Dishman/Getty Images

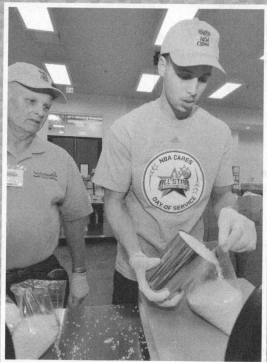

Jesse D. Garrabrant/Getty Images

When he's not on the court, Stephen pursues charitable interests. Here, he volunteers at a food bank as part of the 2013 NBA Cares All-Star Weekend.

Both Stephen and his brother, Seth Curry, play in the NBA. Here, Stephen maneuvers around his brother in a game against the Dallas Mavericks.

After a game against the Atlanta Hawks, Stephen and his father, Dell Curry, talk basketball on the court. Both father and son have played professionally.

Stephen visits with fans during a community event at his old school to celebrate the Golden State Warriors' victory in the 2015 NBA Finals.

Stephen goes for a trey as opposing players close in.
His unique style makes his three-pointers hard
to block.

Stephen jumps up to score against one of his toughest competitors, LeBron James.

Ezra Shaw/Getty Images

# Stephen Curry Year-to-Year Highlights:

**2005:**
- North Carolina All-State
- Bojangles' Shootout tournament MVP

**2006:**
- North Carolina All-State
- Bojangles' Shootout tournament MVP
- Chick-fil-A Classic tournament MVP
- State finals runner-up

**2007:**
- Set Davidson College freshman points record
- Southern Conference champion
- Southern Conference tournament Most Outstanding Player
- Southern Conference Freshman of the Year
- Silver medal, U-19 FIBA World Championship

**2008:**
- Consensus second team All-America
- Southern Conference champion
- Set single-season NCAA three-point field goal record
- ESPY Best Breakthrough Athlete nominee
- Southern Conference Player of the Year
- Southern Conference tournament Most Outstanding Player
- Southern Conference Male Athlete of the Year (all sports)
- Wooden Award finalist
- CollegeInsider.com Mid-Major Player of the Year

**2009:**
- Consensus first team All-America
- Southern Conference Player of the Year
- Set single-season Davidson College points record
- Set single-season Davidson College steals record
- First-round NBA draft pick

**2010:**
- Gold medal, FIBA World Championship
- NBA All-Rookie First Team
- NBA Rookie of the Year runner-up

**2011:**
- NBA Skills Challenge winner
- NBA Sportsmanship Award

**2012 (injured)**

**2013:**
- Set NBA single-season three-point field goal record
- Led Warriors in scoring and assists

**2014:**
- NBA All-Star
- All-NBA Second Team
- Gold medal, FIBA World Championship
- Led NBA in three-point field goals made

**2015:**
- NBA Most Valuable Player
- NBA Champion
- ESPY Best Male Athlete
- ESPY Best NBA Player
- All-NBA First Team
- Set NBA single-season three-point field goal record

**2016:**
- NBA Most Valuable Player
- First unanimous MVP
- 50-40-90 club
- Led the NBA in scoring
- Led the NBA in steals
- Set NBA single-season three-point field goal record

# Stephen Curry's NBA Statistics

| YEAR | TEAM | G | GS | MIN | PTS | FGM | FGA | FG% | 3PM | 3PA | 3P% | FTM | FTA | FT% | OREB | DREB | REB | AST | STL | BLK | TOV | PF |
|------|------|---|----|----|----|----|----|----|----|----|----|----|----|----|----|----|----|----|----|----|----|----|
| 09-10 | GSW | 80 | 77 | 36.2 | 17.5 | 6.6 | 14.3 | 46.2 | 2.1 | 4.8 | 43.7 | 2.2 | 2.5 | 88.5 | 0.6 | 3.9 | 4.5 | 5.9 | 1.9 | 0.2 | 3.0 | 3.2 |
| 10-11 | GSW | 74 | 74 | 33.6 | 18.6 | 6.8 | 14.2 | 48.0 | 2.0 | 4.6 | 44.2 | 2.9 | 3.1 | 93.4 | 0.7 | 3.2 | 3.9 | 5.8 | 1.5 | 0.3 | 3.1 | 3.1 |
| 11-12 | GSW | 26 | 23 | 28.1 | 14.7 | 5.6 | 11.4 | 49.0 | 2.1 | 4.7 | 45.5 | 1.5 | 1.8 | 80.9 | 0.6 | 2.8 | 3.4 | 5.3 | 1.5 | 0.3 | 2.5 | 2.4 |
| 12-13 | GSW | 78 | 78 | 38.2 | 22.9 | 8.0 | 17.8 | 45.1 | 3.5 | 7.7 | 45.3 | 3.4 | 3.7 | 90.0 | 0.8 | 3.3 | 4.0 | 6.9 | 1.6 | 0.2 | 3.1 | 2.5 |
| 13-14 | GSW | 78 | 78 | 36.5 | 24.0 | 8.4 | 17.7 | 47.1 | 3.3 | 7.9 | 42.4 | 3.9 | 4.5 | 88.5 | 0.6 | 3.7 | 4.3 | 8.5 | 1.6 | 0.2 | 3.8 | 2.5 |
| 14-15 | GSW | 80 | 80 | 32.7 | 23.8 | 8.2 | 16.8 | 48.7 | 3.6 | 8.1 | 44.3 | 3.9 | 4.2 | 91.4 | 0.7 | 3.6 | 4.3 | 7.7 | 2.0 | 0.2 | 3.1 | 2.0 |
| 15-16 | GSW | 79 | 79 | 34.2 | 30.1 | 10.2 | 20.2 | 50.4 | 5.1 | 11.2 | 45.4 | 4.6 | 5.1 | 90.8 | 0.9 | 4.6 | 5.4 | 6.7 | 2.1 | 0.2 | 3.3 | 2.0 |
| 16-17 | GSW | 62 | 62 | 33.6 | 24.9 | 8.4 | 18.1 | 46.3 | 4.0 | 9.9 | 39.9 | 4.2 | 4.6 | 90.8 | 0.7 | 3.7 | 4.5 | 6.3 | 1.8 | 0.2 | 2.9 | 2.3 |
| Totals | | 557 | 551 | 34.7 | 22.7 | 8.0 | 16.7 | 47.5 | 3.3 | 7.6 | 43.7 | 3.5 | 3.8 | 90.3 | 0.7 | 3.7 | 4.4 | 6.8 | 1.8 | 0.2 | 3.2 | 2.5 |

*Stats as of March 8, 2017

# Career Playoff Totals

| YEAR | TEAM | G | GS | MIN | PTS | FGM | FGA | FG% | 3PM | 3PA | 3P% | FTM | FTA | FT% | OREB | DREB | REB | AST | STL | BLK | TOV | PF |
|------|------|---|----|-----|-----|-----|-----|-----|-----|-----|-----|-----|-----|-----|------|------|-----|-----|-----|-----|-----|-----|
| 12-13 | GSW | 12 | 12 | 41.4 | 23.4 | 8.5 | 19.6 | 43.4 | 3.5 | 8.8 | 39.6 | 2.9 | 3.2 | 92.1 | 0.4 | 3.4 | 3.8 | 8.1 | 1.7 | 0.2 | 3.3 | 2.5 |
| 13-14 | GSW | 7 | 7 | 42.4 | 23.0 | 7.3 | 16.6 | 44.0 | 3.1 | 8.1 | 38.6 | 5.3 | 6.0 | 88.1 | 0.6 | 3.0 | 3.6 | 8.4 | 1.7 | 0.1 | 3.7 | 2.6 |
| 14-15 | GSW | 21 | 21 | 39.3 | 28.3 | 9.5 | 20.9 | 45.6 | 4.7 | 11.0 | 42.2 | 4.6 | 5.5 | 83.5 | 1.0 | 4.0 | 5.0 | 6.4 | 1.9 | 0.1 | 3.9 | 2.2 |
| 15-16 | GSW | 18 | 17 | 34.1 | 25.1 | 8.2 | 18.8 | 43.8 | 4.4 | 11.0 | 40.4 | 4.2 | 4.6 | 91.6 | 0.8 | 4.7 | 5.5 | 5.2 | 1.4 | 0.3 | 4.2 | 2.2 |
| Totals |  | 58 | 57 | 38.5 | 25.7 | 8.6 | 19.4 | 44.4 | 4.2 | 10.2 | 40.8 | 4.2 | 4.8 | 87.8 | 0.7 | 4.0 | 4.7 | 6.6 | 1.7 | 0.2 | 3.8 | 2.4 |

# Turn the page to start reading another true basketball story

MATT CHRISTOPHER

The #1 Sports Series for Kids

ON THE COURT WITH . . .

## LeBron James

# ★ PROLOGUE ★

To look at him now, you might not think that LeBron James was once like lots of kids in the United States. But he was. He went to school, played sports, and hung out with his friends. He did chores. He watched television and played video games. He worshipped sports heroes such as Michael Jordan.

LeBron was like many kids in the U.S. in other ways, too. His mother was a single working woman struggling to make ends meet. He never knew his father. Throughout much of his childhood, he lived in neighborhoods where crime, violence, and drug use were the norm.

Yet he was different, too. For one thing, he was tall, taller than most other boys his age. But it was when he picked up a basketball and strode onto the court that his true difference emerged — for that young boy could do things with a basketball that few others could.

Still can.

# ⋆ CHAPTER ONE ⋆

## 1984-1987

### Hickory Street

LeBron James was born on December 30, 1984. His mother, Gloria James, was a sixteen-year-old high school student and unmarried. No one has ever known for certain who his father was.

LeBron and Gloria lived with her mother, Freda, and Gloria's two brothers, Terry and Curt, in a small house on Hickory Street in Akron, Ohio. Hickory Street was in one of Akron's poorer neighborhoods. Sometimes, homes in such areas can fall into disrepair. The neighborhoods themselves can become crime-ridden and dangerous.

Not so with Hickory Street. The residents there kept their homes neat. If a person or family was in need, neighbors stepped forward with food, shelter, clothes, or other help. The people there may not have had much, but what they had they were glad to share, because they knew that someday, they might be the ones who needed help.

Freda, Gloria, Terry, and even Curt, who was only nine when Gloria's baby was born, worked hard to give LeBron all the love and care he needed. It wasn't easy, for money was tight and newborns can be challenging. But they made it work all the same.

They soon had another set of hands to help out. When LeBron was eight months old, Gloria began dating a man named Eddie Jackson. Eddie was twenty years old and struggling to find his direction in life. Freda helped him by giving him a place in her home with her children and grandson.

Not all twenty-year-old men are comfortable around babies, but Eddie took to LeBron right away. In fact, he is the only man LeBron has ever called Dad.

LeBron quickly grew from an infant to an active toddler. Jumping, running, tackling — he was in constant motion. "You could be laying on the floor," Eddie once recalled, "and the next thing you know . . . he'd jump right on you."

So much energy needed an outlet. So, for Christmas just before LeBron's third birthday, Eddie and Gloria purchased a child-sized basketball hoop and ball. They set it up near the tree on Christmas Eve.

But that night, tragedy struck. Around three o'clock, Freda James collapsed in her kitchen. Eddie heard her fall and came running. He shouted for Gloria to call for help. But it was too late. Freda died in his arms within minutes.

Gloria, Eddie, Terry, and Curt were grief-stricken. Yet with great effort, they hid their sorrow from little LeBron that Christmas morning.

"We wanted to make things as normal for him as possible," Eddie later said. "He had no idea that his grandmother had died."

Indeed, photographs they took that day show LeBron laughing and enjoying the wonder of the holiday. They also show him playing with his brand-new basketball set. At first, he didn't really know how to use it properly. Instead of tossing the ball into the hoop, he rammed it through the rim with fierce slam dunks.

Gloria and Eddie raised the hoop to its highest level, thinking it would encourage LeBron to try shooting. Instead, as the family watched half amused, half amazed, LeBron simply took a running leap and stuffed the ball.

"I was thinking, 'Man, this kid has some elevation for just being three years old,'" Eddie remembered.

LeBron's happiness that Christmas morning was a welcome distraction from the grief the others were feeling over Freda's death. But when the holidays were over, the reality of their loss and their situation set in.

Freda had been the glue that held the family together. Without her, things slowly fell apart.

Eddie, Terry, and Gloria, scarcely more than children themselves, struggled to take care of twelve-year-old Curt and three-year-old LeBron. Their Hickory Street neighbors helped with meals and child care, but there was only so much they could do. And there was nothing anyone could do to help the James children overcome their grief.

As for the house, none of them had the time, money, or know-how to properly care for it. Before long, the dwelling fell into disrepair. Then the city had it condemned — and eventually torn down.

Without a roof over their heads, Gloria, LeBron, and the others were forced to search for other places to live — or else take to the streets, homeless.

# ✷ CHAPTER TWO ✷

## 1987–1994

## LeBron and Gloria

In the wake of Freda's death and the loss of the Hickory Street house, the James family had no choice but to split up. Terry and Curt left together to find a new place to live. Eddie, who was no longer dating Gloria, moved in with his aunt.

Gloria and LeBron, meanwhile, moved to Elizabeth Park. Elizabeth Park was located in a rough, crime-ridden area where the wail of police sirens often woke residents in the middle of the night.

"I saw drugs, guns, killings," LeBron later recalled. "It was crazy."

But Elizabeth Park was also where many of Gloria's friends lived, people who opened their homes to her and her son. Gloria couldn't afford a place of her own, so when someone offered them a room to sleep in, she accepted gratefully.

They didn't stay with one set of friends for more than a few months, however. "My mom would always say,

'Don't get comfortable, because we may not be here long,'" LeBron remembered, adding that when he was five years old, they moved seven times.

Adjusting to such an unsettled existence wasn't easy for either of them. But somehow, Gloria managed to make it work. "My mom kept food in my mouth and clothes on my back," LeBron said years later.

Not surprisingly, LeBron found the violence in and around Elizabeth Park terrifying. Equally frightening was the fact that youngsters not much older than him were sometimes involved in the crimes.

But he himself never got in trouble. "That just wasn't me," he has said. "I knew it was wrong."

LeBron didn't have many close friends back then because he and Gloria moved around so much. Attending school regularly was difficult for him, too. In fact, when he was in the fourth grade, he missed more than eighty days of school!

Fortunately, around this same time, LeBron found a new lifeline in the form of organized sports. In 1994, he joined a football team, the South Rangers, in Akron's Pee Wee League. Attending practices, learning the rules, playing the game, making friends — nine-year-old LeBron loved everything about football and being part of a team.

"The South Rangers meant a lot to me," he said. "All

the coaches and the parents really cared about us. I actually wanted to play in the NFL."

Such a dream wasn't that far-fetched, for LeBron was a terrific player, one whose prowess on the field got him attention.

Frankie Walker Sr. was one of the people who noticed LeBron. Walker had once played for the South Rangers himself and still enjoyed following his old team's schedule. He befriended LeBron and Gloria. When he learned about LeBron's long absences from school, he realized the pair's erratic home life was causing trouble for the youngster.

Walker didn't want LeBron to be one of those kids who fell through the cracks, so he approached Gloria with an unusual proposal. He, his wife, Pam, and their three children wanted LeBron to come live with them.

It was to be a temporary situation, he assured Gloria, just until she was settled somewhere. If she agreed, LeBron would be treated as a member of their family. He would have regular meals, a structured schedule that included attending school regularly and doing household chores, plus the comfort of a nice home and the support of people who cared about him.

Gloria saw that the Walkers were good people and that LeBron liked and trusted them as much as she did.

So, with the knowledge that she and LeBron would be together most weekends, she agreed to let LeBron go live with the Walkers.

The arrangement proved life-changing for LeBron. Under the Walkers' care, he settled into a routine that provided him with more stability than he had ever known.

"They are like my family," LeBron says today, "and I wouldn't be here without them."

It was while living with the Walkers that he returned to a sport he'd first tried when he was just two years old: basketball.

# ⋆ INTRODUCTION ⋆

## Air Jordan

Michael Jordan defied the law of gravity.

At least that's what opponents, teammates, and fans claimed. From the time he first burst upon the scene as a freshman at the University of North Carolina to his final game with the Washington Wizards, he soared high above the rest. Of all the basketball players in the world, few have come close to his level of talent.

So what was it about Michael Jordan's play that made him so special? The answer is simple: Every time he touched the basketball, there was a good chance he would do something with it no one had ever seen done before.

Get him the ball at the top of the key and maybe he'd launch himself from the free throw line, lift the ball high above his head, and make a thunderous jam through the hoop.

Feed him a pass near the basket and he might leap up and seem to hang in the air as defenders tried — unsuccessfully — to knock the ball from his hand. Then, as he finally started to come down, he'd casually flip the ball underhand toward the basket, where it would kiss the glass and fall through for two more points.

Perhaps he'd take the ball to the hoop himself — not for a simple lay-up, however. Instead, as defenders tried to stop him, he'd start on one side of the basket, jump, spin 360 degrees through the air, come out on the other side, flick the ball over his head, and catch nothing but net.

The great plays weren't ever the same twice. But the look after the plays became one that any basketball follower would recognize. Sweat glistening off his shaved head. Mouth wide open. Tongue curled around his lower lip. It all added up to classic Michael Jordan.

But you'd better not blink because the whole thing would only take seconds from start to finish. Then

Michael Jordan would be in motion again, a look of wild surprise upon his face as the crowd roared and his opponents rolled their eyes and shook their heads. Often, he would flash a quick smile as if to say, "How about that?" and then glance up toward his family in the stands before sprinting back up court, ready to do it all once more.

He didn't get the nickname Air Jordan for nothing, after all.

But Michael Jordan wasn't born with the ability to play basketball better than any other human being on the planet. When he first started playing, he couldn't dribble the ball without bouncing it off his foot. His shots didn't even make it to the basket. And dunking a basketball? That was just a dream!

So how did Michael Jordan become so good?

He knew people aren't born great athletes; they make themselves great athletes. Through hard work, practice, and determination, the best athletes learn to take advantage of their physical gifts and develop them to the fullest. Great players love competition and always strive to become better.

That is how Michael Jordan became perhaps the greatest basketball player of all time. He was blessed with tremendous physical skill, true enough, but he also worked extremely hard throughout his career to develop the talent he was born with. Each time he failed, he tried again and tried harder. Each time he succeeded, he gave himself another goal to strive toward.

"I never felt the desire to rest on what I had accomplished," he once said.

Considering what he accomplished, and the indelible mark those accomplishments have left on the sport of basketball, those are powerful words. Almost as powerful as the man who said them.

# GET ON THE FIELD, UNDER THE NET, AND BEHIND THE PLATE WITH YOUR FAVORITE ALL-STARS!

Read the entire Great Americans in Sports series by
## MATT CHRISTOPHER

LB-KIDS.COM

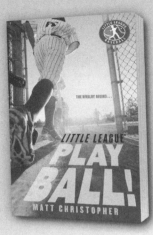
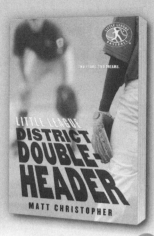

# TWO PLAYERS, ONE DREAM...
## to win the Little League Baseball® World Series

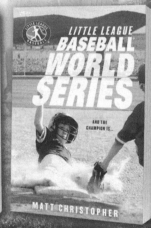

Read all about Carter's and Liam's journeys in the Little League series
by **MATT CHRISTOPHER.**

 **LITTLE, BROWN AND COMPANY**
BOOKS FOR YOUNG READERS

Discover more at lb-kids.com